The Evolution of Spatial
Competence

The Evolution of Spatial Competence

THOMAS WYNN

Illinois Studies in Anthropology
No. 17

UNIVERSITY OF ILLINOIS PRESS

Urbana and Chicago

© 1989 by the Board of Trustees of the University of Illinois
Manufactured in the United States of America
P   5   4   3   2   1

This book is printed on acid-free paper.

Library of Congress Cataloging-in-Publication Data

Wynn, Thomas Grant, 1949–
     The evolution of spatial competence / Thomas G. Wynn.
        p.   cm. -- (Illinois studies in anthropology ; no. 17)
     Bibliography: p.
     Includes index.
     ISBN 0-252-06030-X
     1. Space perception--History.   2. Intellect--History.   3. Genetic
psychology.   4. Fossil man.   I. Title.   II. Series.
     BF469.W96   1989
     155.7--dc 19   88-17110
                                                                            CIP

Contents

General Introduction

This book is about two subjects, the evolution of spatial thinking and the evolution of human intelligence. The first subject is the easier of the two to define and to study. It is intrinsically interesting, I think, especially to anyone who found high school geometry to be "obvious" or who enjoys the unfolded boxes on intelligence tests. Spatial thinking is something we do every day, and as a species we are remarkably good at it. It has clearly evolved and so is, in and of itself, worthy of attention. Intelligence is a vaguer idea altogether. We "know" that we are more intelligent than chimpanzees and that this difference is somehow important to human success, but it is a difficult concept to define and an even more difficult concept to study in human evolution. This book looks at the evolution of intelligence by tracing the development of spatial thinking, just one of the behaviors we often consider to be intelligent.

This is an archaeology book written by an archaeologist. Geometry and spatial thinking can be studied mathematically and from the perspective of psychology, to name just two disciplines interested in space. I draw on both of these kinds of spatial analysis, quite heavily at times, but my interest is more in line with an archaeological worldview. How did our ancestors think about space in their everyday lives? How did these notions of space change? What do spatial abilities tell us about the overall behavior of our predecessors? Archaeology is by nature an optimistic discipline that strives to build an understanding of the past out of small and fragmented pieces. I share that optimism and in this book present both steps of archaeological thinking—a detailed analysis of the pieces, in this case the geometry of stone tools, and a general interpretation of past behavior, the evolution of intelligence.

My theoretical grounding is unabashedly, but not uncritically, Piagetian. My discussion of the evolution of human intelligence is based upon Piaget's scheme of intellectual development, especially the categories of intelligence that are his stages. I do not, however, naively apply Piaget's entire developmental program to human phylogeny; I am especially suspicious of his vision of phylogenetic mechanism. Despite its weaknesses in some areas when compared to other prevailing theories of development, Piagetian theory has certain advantages in a study of this kind. Perhaps most important is its treatment of space. Piaget and Barbel Inhelder devoted considerable attention to the development of spatial concepts, and these results can be applied, with little modification, to stone tools. I know of no other theory of development that attends to space so closely. In addition, a Piagetian analysis can be used on relatively small samples, and such are the basis of most Stone Age archaeology. In the actual analysis I have tried to stay away from Piaget's general interpretations and theoretical argument. I do rely to some extent on the results of experiments on children's spatial abilities done by Piaget and Inhelder (1967). But I have also used basic geometry texts as a source for the spatial categories of the analysis—proximity, congruency, and so on. The Piagetian content of the analysis is as atheoretical as I could make it, given my acknowledged background in Piagetian scholarship. Just as Piaget's experimental results can be interpreted from alternative general theories, so too can my assessment of tool geometry (see Atran 1982 for a good example).

The book is divided into two parts. The first part contains an analysis of the spatial competence of early hominids, using the geometry of stone tools as evidence. The analysis itself is organized according to three categories of geometric relationship—topological, projective, and euclidean. Part I concludes with a chronologically arranged summary of the evolution of spatial competence and a brief discussion of what I consider to be its two major developments. Part II contains the discussion of the evolution of intelligence. It begins with a brief summary of relevant aspects of Piagetian theory, followed by a chronological summary of the evolution of human intelligence from the Piagetian perspective.

Acknowledgments

I would like to thank Dr. Mary Leakey, the staff of the National Museum of Tanzania, and the staff of the Kenya National Museum for their assistance in the initial analysis of the artifacts.

I would also like to thank Sally McBrearty and Jean Bell for the line drawings and Elaine Schantz for manuscript preparation.

Many people have contributed valuable criticism in the development of my thinking. Foremost among them are Charles Keller and Eugene Giles and, much earlier, Scott Littleton.

PART I:

The Evolution of Intuitive Geometries

Introduction

Spatial thinking is one of the most basic tasks of the animal mind. In order to move about, locate itself, locate food, shelter, and mates, an animal must have some understanding of space. From the perspective of evolutionary biology, spatial competence can be viewed as an important facet of an animal's niche. Because of this, we should expect differing understandings of space. Certainly a dolphin's understanding of space must be very different from that of a horse. Spatial thinking is an important feature of primate niches, where the ability to move about in the tops of tropical trees has selected for both perceptual and cognitive components. Spatial thinking is also an important component of human thinking. We use it to build dams, fly to the moon, plan the drive to work, and throw baseballs. This spatial competence has evolved; our abstract notions of dimensional space, even "simple" euclidean space, are certainly different from anything we know of the spatial competence of our nearest relatives. While spatial thinking may not be *the* key to the evolution of human thinking, it may be a window through which we can glimpse the evolution of the hominid mind.

The first half of this book addresses the evolution of hominid "intuitive" geometries. In order to act, hominids had to have some understanding of spatial relationships. These could be as simple as "next to" or as complex as "bearing 67°, range 10,000 meters." Some notions of space are obviously simpler than others. Intuitive geometries consist of cognitive strategies used to arrange action in space. They are commonsense tools used for real-world tasks. As such they require no reflection upon the nature of space or conscious reasoning of any sort (though this is not ruled out). Intuitive geometries need not be coherent theories of space in order to be real and usable in the everyday world. Indeed, one learns them through experience in the everyday world—hence the term "intuitive" geometries. Despite the modifier, these spatial notions do represent spatial relationships that can be formalized in modern, mathematical geometry. Proximity, projection, and symmetry, for example, can easily be found in geometry texts. However, they are also intuitive understandings of spatial relationships, and, as I hope to show, these intuitions have evolved over the course of the last two million years of hominid evolution.

The analysis itself follows sections on method and sample. It is organized according to types of spatial relations. The division is one of convenience; I do not mean to suggest that hominids compartmentalized their spatial thinking in such a fashion. Topology, projective geometry, and euclidean geometry are all fields of formalized geometry and as such are at least vaguely familiar to readers. These types of space supply the analysis with well-defined and internally coherent sets of spatial concepts. I thought it best to maintain this coherence, at least initially.

Method

How can one obtain information about the spatial competence of hominids dead for hundreds of thousands, even millions, of years? It is clear we cannot interview them, read their treatises on geometry, or give them psychometric tests. We have only what they have left behind, a mélange of garbage, abandoned camps, and broken and discarded tools. Like all archaeologists, though, I find this refuse remarkably informative. From it we can, in fact, get a glimpse of early hominids' intuitive geometries.

All of the evidence in this book comes from stone tools. Unfortunately, stone is not an ideal medium. One cannot work one's will on it as easily as one can carve wood or mold clay. But the former rarely preserves and the latter makes its appearance only very, very late in prehistory. We do have some possible dwellings from the early Stone Age—patterns of posts, floors of cobbles, and the like, which are potentially useful in a study such as this. But, again until very late, the nature of these structures is controversial. More to the point, however, their patterns, even if reliable, tell us no more than we know from the stone tools. We have stone tools in the millions, from almost every point in time over the last two million years. Most are in much the same condition as when discarded by their prehistoric maker. They constitute our most abundant and well-preserved pieces of fossilized behavior.

Fracturing stones yields sharp edges; this is the basic principle of much of Stone Age technology. In prehistory, this was usually a matter of breaking small pieces (flakes) off of larger chunks (cores). Both flakes and cores have sharp edges and both were used as tools by early hominids. Stone knapping is a subtractive task; one removes material to achieve a result. By removing small flakes (trimming flakes) the knapper can control the shape of core and flake tools. The result is a wide range of shapes and edge configurations that can be used for a correspondingly wide range of tasks. But there are limitations. While immense amounts of time (and metal tools!) will produce a *David* out of marble, pragmatic stone knapping is not so versatile. The nature of the stone and economy of production constrain the freedom of expression. Even though the Stone Age presents us with some strikingly beautiful tools, most are modest accomplishments that took only a few moments to make and that were likely discarded a few moments later. Nevertheless, they did require attention, however fleeting, and from this attention we can recover something of the knapper's intuitive geometry.

In order to investigate spatial concepts from stone tools, one must first identify patterns that were clearly intentional. Much that is regular about stone tools is purely accidental. The physics of stone knapping and the petrology of certain kinds of stone will together often produce parallel edges, trapezoidal cross sections, and symmetries, to name just a few. Of course these cannot be used as evidence for a knapper's spatial repertoire because they could have been fortuitous. The best indication we have of intention comes from secondary trimming. If a knapper modified a core or flake by removing more pieces from it, we can assume that he intended to do so and, moreover, that he used spatial concepts of some sort to guide his action. Intention does not require some sophisticated image or mental template, though in some cases these may have been operative; it can be as simple as knapping off a flake or two in order to remove an unwanted projection. However, even such a simple modification requires some notions of space. The analyses in this book concern, therefore, the patterns of trimming found on tools. Occasionally they also consider the overall shape of the artifact, but only in cases where it is clearly the result of extensive trimming.

The actual technique of analysis is neither sophisticated nor especially remarkable. I examined all of the artifacts from each assemblage and chose those I judged to represent the most sophisticated spatial competences. Because I am interested only in the spatial competences of the hominids I have not considered the nature of the entire assemblages nor described the range of artifacts in each. Such a qualitative technique may appear sacrilegious in this age of indices and computer analysis, but there is a sound reason for it: quantification would accomplish nothing. Counting the number of artifacts requiring a certain competence would reveal no more about that competence than would describing three or four representative examples. Further, it is reasonable to describe only the most informative artifacts because the focus of the analysis is on the most sophisticated competences of any assemblage. Tools made by juveniles (and we must assume that many of the artifacts in our collections were), for example, would not represent the most sophisticated competence and are of no use to a phylogenetic study. Similarly, a lengthy analysis of waste flakes would yield no useful information because their shape, at least until very late in prehistory, was not intentional. I did try to avoid unique examples. Even though a remarkable pattern or configuration seemed, at least to me, certainly intentional, it remained just possible that it was an accident. However, if this pattern was repeated on another artifact, I decided that the possibility of its being an accident was reduced to an acceptably low level, and felt comfortable in including it in the sample. There are only two or three such unusual patterns in the study.

The analysis does not use any standard archaeological typology. I do use some archaeological terms such as "scraper" and "handaxe" but only as convenient terms of reference. The implied function in such terms is irrelevant. Indeed, the purpose for which the hominid made the tools is not at issue. Nor are differences between contemporary assemblages or even associated artifacts relevant. A hominid could have made two tools with very different tasks in mind, but if he used the same spatial notions to conceive both of them, then, from the point of view of this analysis, the tools are equivalent. There is a typology of sorts inherent in the analysis. It consists solely of spatial relationships identified on the tools—proximity and symmetry, for example. Compared to many archaeological analyses the range of types is rather narrow and the resulting classification, if it can even be called that, very "lumpy." But it is not my intention to explain all archaeological variation, only that which informs us about the spatial competence of the artisans; and, as we shall see, the scheme that I use does nicely.

One last methodological issue needs to be addressed—the problem of minimum necessary competence. This problem is a direct consequence of the paucity of the archaeological record. We see only a very narrow range of hominid behavior, including spatial behavior. Is it not possible that hominids used their most sophisticated spatial concepts in realms other than stone knapping? It is difficult to get around this problem. Indeed, we can never logically eliminate the possibility that a two-million-year-old Euclid made crude stone tools while drawing triangles in the sand. Any characterization of spatial repertoire represents the bare minimum, that is, what the hominid had to have understood in order to conceive the tool. As a consequence, the analysis risks underestimating abilities. By the same token it is, I think, impossible to *overestimate* abilities.

The Archaeological Sample

For this analysis I have chosen a sample of stone tools from sites that span about 1.5 million years of hominid evolution. From the earliest Olduvai tools to the fine handaxes from Isimila, the sample encompasses the first 85 percent of known archaeological time. However, the sample does not present a continuous sequence. Rather, it is constructed from several "flashes" in time, each consisting of a site or sites, whose relative chronological positions are fairly well established. The temporal gaps between these flashes are very large, and undoubtedly conceal developments of direct relevance to our problem. Unfortunately, we must take the archaeological record as it is found and make do. The relative dating of the samples is based on chronometric determinations and stratigraphic relationships, and, while certain dates are more reliable than others, the overall precision of the chronology is adequate for the purpose at hand. The sites fall into three groups whose relative ages are clear (Table 1). The first group includes four sites from Bed I and lower Bed II at Olduvai Gorge: DK, FLK, FLK N, and HWK East level 2. These date to between 1.8 and 1.6 million years ago (hereafter, "mya") (Hay 1976). The second group includes sites from upper Bed II at Olduvai—HWK East level 4, EFHR, SHK, and BK—and also the MHS and RHS localities from West Natron, Tanzania. These date to between 1.5 and 1.0 mya (Isaac 1967; Hay 1976). The third group includes artifacts from two levels, sands 1 and sands 3, at the Isimila prehistoric site, also in Tanzania. These date to about 300,000 years ago (Howell et al. 1962). A more detailed discussion of the chronology follows.

The earliest group of sites constitutes a relative sequence within Bed I and lower Bed II at Olduvai. Bed I, as defined by Hay (1976), includes the entire sequence of tuffs and clays between the Naabi ignimbrite and Bed II. The archaeological deposits of Bed I span a period from about 1.7 to 1.8 mya, a duration of only about 100,000 years. This date is based primarily on the high reliability of potassium

Dates	Samples		Industries	
present				
	★			
	★			
300,000	Isimila			
	★			
	★			
			A	
			c	
			h	
			e	
			u	
			l	
			e	
1,000,000			a D 0	
	BK	★	n e l	
	B	★	. v d	
	E SHK	★	e o	
	D EFHR	West Natron	l w	
		★	o a	
	II HWK East 4	★	p n	
		★	e	
			d	
1,500,000	HWK East 2		0	
			l	
	B FLK N		d	
	E		o	
	D FLK		w	
			a	
	I DK		n	
2,000,000				

Table 1

argon dates from one of the marker tuffs, Tuff IB (1.79 ± 03). The archaeological sites of DK, FLK, and FLK N are superposed stratigraphically within Bed I: DK, the earliest locality at Olduvai, lies below Tuff IB; FLK, the "Zinjanthropus" floor, lies between Tuff IB and Tuff IC; and FLK N lies just below Tuff IF, which marks the top of the Bed I sequence.

Bed II is divided by a disconformity into two units. The lower unit, between Tuff IF and the disconformity, resembles Bed I in lithology and faunal content more than it does the upper part of Bed II. The disconformity has been dated at about 1.60 mya (Hay 1976), based primarily on palaeomagnetic data rather than potassium argon dates, which are unsatisfactory. The site of HWK East contains several artifact-bearing horizons, two of which I have used in this study. Level 2 lies stratigraphically between Tuff IF and the disconformity, and level 4 lies just above the disconformity. The HWK East level 2 artifacts therefore date to somewhere between 1.70 mya (top of I) and 1.65 mya, the age of the disconformity. Taken as a whole, then, the stratigraphic sequence of DK, FLK, FLK N, and HWK East level 2 represents a duration of no more than 200,000 years.

The top of Bed II has been estimated by Hay (1976) to date to about 1.15 mya. This date is not a direct chronometric measurement but was inferred from relative stratal thickness, faulting associated with an elsewhere-dated phase of Rift Valley faulting, and potassium argon dates from Bed IV. The sites of HWK East level 4, EFHR, SHK, and BK lie stratigraphically between the disconformity and the top of Bed II. Within this 450,000-year time span, HWK East 4 is the earliest. Sites SHK and EFHR are later and roughly contemporaneous (stratigraphically), and BK is the most recent of the four sites. It should be noted that the span of geologic time represented by these sites may be more than double the span represented by the sites from Bed I and lower Bed II.

The Peninj group from West Natron has been divided into the Moinik and Humbu formations, the former occurring conformably above the latter wherever both are found (Isaac 1967). Two archaeological sites, MHS and RHS, were located in upper deposits of the Humbu formation, above a basalt designated the WaMbugu basalt. Because the sites occur in separate localities their relative ages are impossible to determine. However, the general age of the deposit in which both occur has been determined from potassium argon and palaeomagnetic data. Two consistent potassium argon runs have been made on the intra-Moinik basalt which *overlies* the archaeological horizons (Isaac and Curtis 1974), yielding a mean date of 1.35 mya. The polarity of the samples was indeterminate (apparently the deposits had been struck by lightning). The WaMbugu basalt has yielded a series of six potassium argon dates running from 2.27 to .96 mya. However, the two older dates, 2.27 and 1.55 mya, are from samples less altered than those to which the younger dates were assigned. Also, the normal polarity of WaMbugu could only refer to the Olduvai event (1.8–1.65 mya), since the Jaramillo normal event would be too recent (.9 mya), given the dates on the Moinik formation (which are considered to be more reliable than the WaMbugu dates). Isaac (Isaac and Curtis 1974) concludes that the artifact horizons from West Natron must be considered to date from somewhere between 1.0 and 1.5 mya. They are, therefore, at least roughly contemporaneous with the artifacts from above the Bed II disconformity at Olduvai.

The Isimila formation consists of a series of stratified sands, clays, and sandy clays that has been divided into the Lukingi member and the overlying Lisalamagasi member (Cole and Kleindienst 1974). However, the original archaeological nomenclature, which numbers sand units 1–5 from top to bottom, has come into common use, and I will use it here. Several kinds of archaeological occurrences, from diffuse vertical scatters to occupation horizons, are present in the Isimila deposit, making it an extremely rich archaeological locality. In their original publication, Howell, Cole, and Kleindienst (1962) concluded that all the Isimila beds were laid down within a short time span (a few thousand years), and that all variation among the archaeological assemblages reflected activity differences. Later investigators (Hansen and Keller 1971), however, suggested that there is temporal variation between assemblages from the lower sands (3–5) and those from sands 1. For this book, support of either side of the argument is unnecessary, though I do indicate the level from which examples are taken. Uranium-series dating has been used to date bone from sands 4 (Howell et al. 1972). The ^{230}Th age is 260,000 $+70,000$ $-40,000$ while the ^{213}Pa age is $>170,000$. This should be considered a ballpark figure, as the reliability of this technique is problematical. For the purposes of this study, though, it is sufficient.

There is obviously a sizeable chronological gap in the archaeological sequence discussed here. If Isimila is considered to date from somewhere between 330,000 and 170,000 years ago and the top of Bed II at Olduvai at 1.15 mya, this gap is on the order of 800,000 years, a considerable lacuna. Unfortunately, there are few sites that clearly fall within this time span and none between 1.15 mya and 500,000 years ago (approximate age of Olorgesailie—Isaac 1977). Another possible lacuna involves the disconformity within Bed II at Olduvai, the duration of which is uncertain. The beginning is known (around 1.60 mya), but no reliable date is available for the resumption of sedimentation. Leakey (1971) estimates the age of EFHR at 1.2 or 1.3 mya but this is uncertain. It is just possible that the West Natron occurrences fall somewhere within this hiatus.

The Evidence for Topological Concepts

Geometricians often refer to topology as "rubber-sheet" geometry. If one geometric form can be stretched, twisted, or pushed into the shape of another, the forms are topologically equivalent. Such seemingly basic geometric qualities as length, straightness, angle, and parallel are simply irrelevant to the topological nature of a figure. A triangle can be stretched into a square or a circle or a pentagon; they are all topologically equivalent. However, none of these could be stretched into a figure eight without altering the topological surface. Topology deals with very basic and very simple spatial relations— whether a point is inside or outside a boundary, whether two points are connected or not, whether two regions in space are near to one another or not. For example, with regard to the quality of enclosure, figures A and B are equivalent but neither is equivalent to C.

To put it another way, A could be stretched into B but not into C. All topological notions deal with such qualitative relationships. The mathematics of topology can be very complex (formalizing simple notions can be a formidable challenge), but most of the relations can be apprehended intuitively because most are quite simple—though some are simpler than others. A very rudimentary spatial notion is that of "nearness" or "byness"—whether or not elements are located in the vicinity of one another. Another concept is separation— distinguishing one point from another in space, usually by means of a boundary. More complex than these is the notion of a sequence of elements chained together into a series or an order. This concept of order is intuitively more complex because it requires coordinating nearness while maintaining separation and a constant direction.

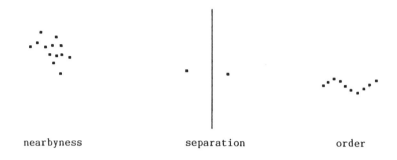

nearbyness   separation   order

Given this intuitive difference in complexity, it seems reasonable to hypothesize that certain topological relations are conceptually more difficult than others and that in any developmental sequence, the simpler relations would be the first to appear. Piaget and Inhelder (1967) have in fact demonstrated this to be true for ontogeny. I hope to show, using stone tools, that it was true in hominid phylogeny as well.

In order to use topological concepts to analyze stone tools we must ask what spatial notions (there had to be some!) the hominid knapper used while striking one stone onto another. We cannot simply use the geometry of the finished product, because almost every stone tool is topologically equivalent—a three-dimensional solid equivalent to a solid ball (the exceptions are stone rings found in some late assemblages). As a consequence we must step down and look at the arrangement of elements on the tool itself. Certain topological relations can be apprehended from the way in which the knapper positioned trimming flakes during the manufacture of an artifact. In a very real sense, the placing of trimming blows, particularly as they are positioned relative to previous ones, reflects concepts used by the knapper.

Three topological notions are especially evident in the trimming patterns of stone tools: proximity, order, and continuity. These represent increasingly complex spatial coordinations. The data concerning proximity consist of artifacts from Bed I Olduvai assemblages that Mary Leakey typed as polyhedrons. Choppers and scrapers, again from Bed I, provide the examples for relations of order, specifically the notions of pair and sequential order. Bifaces from West Natron and Isimila provide the evidence for continuity, the most sophisticated topological notion I will be considering.

Perhaps the most rudimentary spatial concept is that of proximity— the perceiving or placing of elements in the same spatial field. It is simply a notion of "nearness" or "byness," and is so basic that virtually

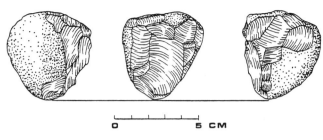

Figure 1

every trimmed artifact is equivalent to every other trimmed artifact. Each trimming blow is in some sense "near" the others on the artifact. The only exceptions are unmodified flakes and cores that have had only one trimming blow or, perhaps, two unrelated trimming blows, though it would be difficult if not impossible to prove that the second trimming flake was not placed somehow near the first. From the perspective of this simple spatial notion all trimmed stone artifacts, from polyhedrons to fine bifacial points, are equivalent because multiple trimming flakes have been placed in proximity to one another. Now there is no known artifact assemblage that consists exclusively of unmodified flakes and single-blow cores. Competence in proximity is, therefore, a kind of base point from which we can begin to describe the evolution of spatial concepts. As it turns out, there are artifacts whose knapper need only have used a notion of proximity. The following examples are from Bed I at Olduvai.

Figure 1 (FLK N). To have made this artifact, the stone knapper need only have struck the cobble repeatedly in the same general vicinity. It was not necessary that he place one blow in some precise relationship to a previous one, only that the blows be more or less near one another. The result was a number of sharp projections and edges that would probably have been useful for several kinds of tasks.

Figure 2 (DK). At first glance this artifact may appear somewhat more sophisticated than the preceding. There are more trimming flakes, removed by blows from several different angles. Simple bashing would not suffice. Because we can only argue about minimum competence, though, we must conclude that this artifact could have been manufactured by someone who simply placed his trimming blows near other trimming blows. I must add that this assessment would be the same whether we considered the artifact a core or a core tool. The minimum spatial competence would not change.

These two artifacts come from separate localities and each was found in the company of more sophisticated artifacts. They do not represent a real archaeological assemblage. Indeed, as stated previ-

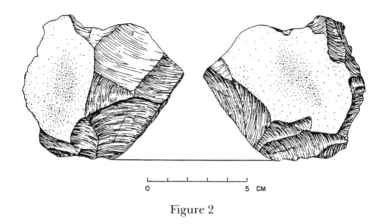

0   5 CM

Figure 2

ously, there is no known assemblage that consists entirely of artifacts of such simplicity. However, it is at least conceivable that an assemblage of such artifacts did in fact constitute the earliest recognizable (though as yet unrecognized) set of stone tools.

The topological relation of order is more complex than that of proximity and indeed coordinates proximity with other relations. While still a relatively simple notion, order is a crucial prerequisite for the manufacture of most kinds of stone tools. Order requires the coordination of proximity and separation, combined with a constant direction of movement. In proximity the elements need not be distinguished from one another; that is, they need not be dissociated into specific entities playing specific roles. They are simply all located near or even on top of one another. This was especially true of the artifact in the first example. Separation is the notion of distinguishing or segregating the elements in a spatial field so that each can have a specific, rather than general, relation to the others. Order coordinates separation with proximity to create such concepts as the pair, the sequence, and, most complex, the reversible sequence.

In a pair, proximity and separation are coordinated but there is no need for a constant direction of movement. The elements in a pair must be distinct yet contiguous, hence the coordination of separation and proximity. The following examples illustrate this concept.

Figure 3 (FLK N). This is a fairly classic Oldowan chopper. Four trimming blows have produced a single sharp edge along about one-third of the circumference of a cobble. Trimming flakes A and B preceded trimming flakes C and D. In effect, the artifact is the result of two pairs of trimming blows. The order of the blows within each pair is irrelevant, as is the order of the pairs to one another. Again, I am emphasizing how the knapper had to place trimming blows to achieve

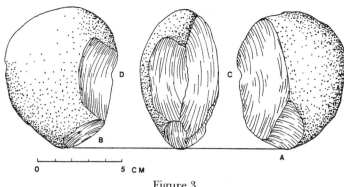

Figure 3

the result. Bashing in a general vicinity would not have been sufficient. The knapper directed three specific blows (dissociation, separation) to a position adjacent to preceding blows (proximity). Indeed,
preceding negative scars appear to have supplied specific striking
platforms for subsequent blows. The result is not a random collection
of projections and edges but a single working edge. The minimum
necessary concept is that of the pair.

Figure 4 (FLK). This is a unifacial chopper, and, even though it is
not a case of a pair of pairs, the minimum competence is the same as
that of the preceding example. After the first blow, the knapper
placed each subsequent blow adjacent to a preceding one. Each blow
was directed by, at the minimum, a coordination of the spatial notions
of separation and proximity. Beyond this notion of pairs there was no
spatial coordination.

Each of the above two examples required a spatial concept more
complex than that of simple "nearbyness." The result of contiguous
placing of trimming blows is a single prominent edge. One could argue that the flake scars of the previous examples of "proximity only"
artifacts (Figures 1 and 2) were also placed contiguously and hence
also represent a rudimentary concept of order. This is possible. However, there is nothing about these more primitive artifacts, such as one
prominent edge, that *required* a concept more sophisticated than simple proximity, and, to reiterate a crucial point, we can only argue
about minimum competence. Contiguous placing of trimming blows
may not seem a very profound development or even much of an advance over simple proximity. Nevertheless, it does represent a coordination of two simple notions—proximity and separation—and it is
coordination, even simple coordination, that is essential to more complex concepts of space. Furthermore, on a more practical level, contiguous placing of trimming blows is a necessary ability for the manu-

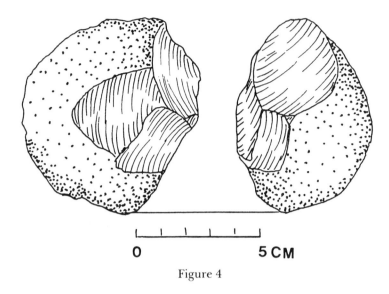

0   5 CM

Figure 4

facture of virtually all stone tools in prehistory. It is a basic but indispensable first step.

Figure 5 (FLK N). This chopper has at least eleven trimming flakes and, at first glance, appears more sophisticated than the preceding two examples. In addition to simple pairs, the single edge on this chopper required that the concept of separation incorporate several elements. This pattern is intuitively more complicated than that of the simple pair. In mathematical topology, separation is often exemplified by points positioned on opposite sides of a boundary of some sort (inside or outside a circle, for example). On the chopper in Figure 5, the knapper produced a sinuous edge by trimming onto two faces of a cobble. True, the placing of each blow required the idea of a pair in space. But the notion of a single edge also acted as a kind of boundary separating the blows from each face of the tool. What makes this more sophisticated than a simple pair is that the boundary—the edge—had to have been maintained for several trimming blows. This boundary was a spatial reference used by the knapper to orient his blows. The concept of a simple pair was not quite sufficient.

The notion of an ordered sequence requires the coordination of proximity and separation with the addition of a constant direction of movement or orientation. A pair is a pair regardless of the directional orientation of the second element to the first. But if we want to create a series of elements, such as a line of posts, we must employ some concept in addition to separation and nearness. We must place the third element and all subsequent elements in some specific spatial re-

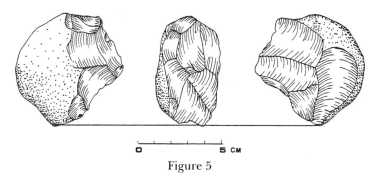

Figure 5

lation to *all* of the preceding elements. We cannot simply place the third post near the second; we must also consider the position of the first. This is most easily done by maintaining a constant direction of movement. This coordination is more complex than that of the pair because several distinct elements (separation) must be related through some concept of arrangement, even one as simple as "move to the left."

Figure 6a (FLK N). In the view shown here, the lower edge of the artifact consists of a series of six unifacial flake scars. On close examination one can see that the knapper did not strike off the trimming flakes one after another in exact sequence (at least one is out of place; see arrow). Consequently, any comparison to a strict sequence such as ABCDEF would be spurious. Nevertheless, the end result is the same—one flake scar following another. The violation of a strict order should not be disturbing. It is unlikely that these early hominids played logical games with themselves, at least using stone tools. The coordination of proximity and order in this artifact is certainly more complex than that of a pair. Each flake is placed in relation not just to another one but to *all* of the other flake scars. The knapper achieved this result by restricting successive trimming blows to a single direction. This constant direction of movement is the third notion in a concept of order.

Figure 6b (DK). Everything said of the preceding example concerning order can also be said of this artifact. The trimming sequence appears to have been from top to bottom, as the artifact is drawn. This example differs from earlier ones in that it is a *flake* tool; that is, the blank itself was a flake rather than a cobble or a chunk of stone. This implies two major manufacturing steps—the removal of the flake from a core and the subsequent trimming of the flake. While this increase in number of steps reflects a greater complexity of sorts, it is of no direct relevance to a discussion of spatial concepts, especially since we have no way of knowing whether the whole sequence was

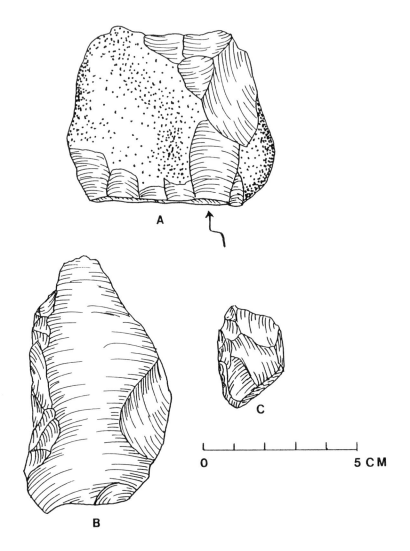

A

B

C

0   5 CM

Figure 6

conceived at the outset or whether the knapper simply selected a pre-viously struck flake as most appropriate for the task at hand. The spatial concepts necessary for trimming this flake are identical to those used on the cobble in the preceding example. The importance of this unifacial flake tool is its occurrence in one of the earliest known archaeological sites.

Figure 6c (FLK N). This small scraper was also made on a flake. The trimming flakes are related to one another in the same manner as those of the two preceding examples. What is important here is the small size of the trimming flakes; the knapper needed a fairly fine motor control to make this artifact. The "primitiveness" of Oldowan tools cannot, therefore, be explained in terms of poor motor coordi-nation on the part of the hominids.

In making these three artifacts, Oldowan hominids employed a spa-tial concept more sophisticated than that of a simple pair. Put ab-stractly, we can argue for a concept of linear order. Each element, in this case trimming flakes, was placed in relation to several other ele-ments, the result being a sequence. Though their order was not as elegant as a purely mathematical series such as ABCDEF, it is still clear that these hominids were capable of arranging a sequence of elements.

The spatial concepts of proximity, separation, pairs, and order ap-pear to exhaust the spatial repertoire of Oldowan stone knappers. These spatial relations are relatively simple but still sufficient to allow manufacture of a range of edge types and tool forms that these homi-nids used to their advantage in processing animals (Potts 1984) and, presumably, plants. However, the simplicity of these spatial concepts does give the Oldowan artifacts a crude and primitive appearance, especially compared to later stone tools that exhibit sophisticated geo-metric patterns more in line with the geometric regularities of mod-ern material culture. The Oldowan tools appear crude primarily be-cause the spatial competence of the knappers was primitive.

In the realm of order there is another relation that is more sophis-ticated and for which there is no evidence in the Oldowan. This is the reversal of a sequence. Topologically, ABCD and DCBA are the same order, only reversed. Unfortunately, there is no way to determine whether or not a hominid was capable of such a reversal with the kinds of sequences we noted in previous examples. Fortunately, there are some kinds of artifacts that required a reversal, though the spatial elements were more abstract than simple trimming flakes. I am refer-ring, of course, to bifaces, whose bilateral symmetry requires the re-versal of order around a midline. ABC/CBA is a symmetry. The manufacture of any symmetrical biface, of which there are several examples in the following pages, requires the ability to reverse an order. True, the sequence that is reversed in a symmetry is one of spatial intervals, itself a complex spatial notion (see below). Nevertheless, it is a reversal of sequence and as such requires a more complex spatial competence than simple order. To put it another way, the coordination of proximity and order in a symmetrical biface is more complex than the order relations required for examples 2–6.

The final topological notion of use in analyzing stone tools is that of continuity—the relationship of parts to a whole. A line is, topologically, an infinite series of indiscernably small points. In order to conceive of a line in this fashion, it is necessary to be able to subdivide the line infinitely and then recreate it in thought from the resulting elements. Stated in another way, one must analyze a whole (the line) into its constituent elements (the points) and resynthesize these elements into the whole. It is a breaking down and putting back together which, in terms of simpler topological relations, requires the coordination of proximity, separation, and order. Such whole-part relations are among the most sophisticated of topological notions and, if we can get at them, should be quite important in characterizing the spatial competence of early hominids. It is obviously impossible to see an infinitely small point or to inquire about understandings of lines. However, it is possible to examine the results of the process of analysis and synthesis, the ability to break a whole into constituent elements and put it back together again. The first of the following examples are the most sophisticated artifacts; after these I will discuss less sophisticated examples. By presenting the best first I hope to show just what I mean by analysis and synthesis in the manufacture of stone tools.

Figure 7 (Isimila, sands 3). The bilateral symmetry of this artifact is relevant at this point only because it appears to have been the goal of the knapper. What is important to the present discussion is the manner in which the knapper achieved the desired shape. The artifact demonstrates what I refer to as "minimal trimming." The knapper achieved a definite shape using a minimal amount of modification. Indeed, if there were any less trimming we would probably not recognize the symmetry of the artifact. For objects such as the choppers and scrapers of previous examples it is impossible to make judgments about minimal trimming because we have little idea of the knapper's intention concerning overall shape, if in fact he had one. But for artifacts with symmetry or regularity of any arbitrary kind we can make such judgments, keeping in mind that they are, in fact, judgments. The symmetry of this particular biface resulted from four short sections of trimming (A, B, C, and D) that are, for the most part, uncon-

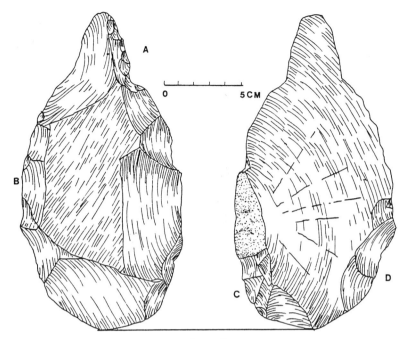

Figure 7

nected with each other. In order to have done this the knapper
needed some notion of the shape broken down into *potential* constituent elements, in this case trimming flakes, and of their combination
into the finished whole—in other words, a fairly sophisticated idea of
the spatial relation of parts to the whole. Only by reducing the shape
to potential trimming flakes could he have determined which were
necessary and which were not. Again, we need not envision the hominid in agonizing contemplation, but even quick, on-the-spot planning
required a notion of whole and parts.

Figure 8 (Isimila, sands 3). There are three sections of trimming on
this cleaver. The trimming differs from that on the preceding example only in that each section has more trimming flakes. The same
kind of analysis and synthesis is still required. The overall shape of
this piece is not symmetrical. Nevertheless, the parallel curves of the
sides suggest a degree of regularity that was probably intentional,
though one cannot, of course, know this with certainty.

I think it is clear that the manufacture of these two artifacts required some understanding of the relation of constituent parts to the
whole. Both artifacts are from the later Acheulean, perhaps 300,000
years old, and the use of such spatial notions at this relatively late date
is perhaps not surprising. Such spatial notions were unnecessary for

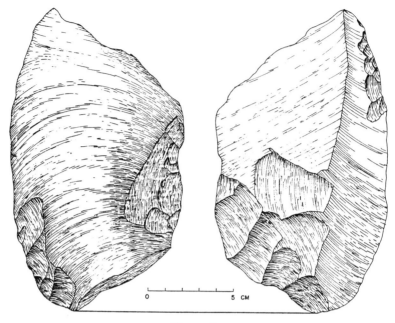

Figure 8

the Oldowan artifacts discussed earlier. There need not have been a notion of a scraping edge, as a whole, made up of constituent elements. Such an edge could be successfully produced using only a competence in order, the placing of trimming flakes in a sequence. Again, this does not exclude the possibility that the maker of the scraper had a more sophisticated competence; it was just not necessary. The question now becomes one of development. Were there transitional forms that demonstrate some rudimentary abilities in the relation of whole to parts? This is a difficult question but there are at least a few artifacts that shed light on the problem.

Figure 9 (West Natron). This biface is from a site considerably older than the two just examined. There is rudimentary symmetry here but it has been achieved in a manner unlike that of the two previous artifacts. This symmetry suggests that some concept of the artifact as a whole was involved. However, the shaping is somewhat haphazard and irregular, at least compared to the later bifaces, and indicates a less sophisticated idea of how flake scars constitute the shape of the piece. It is not clear that all of the trimming flakes play a role in the end result. In other words, even though the trimming appears to have been controlled by notions beyond those of simple proximity and order, they are not as clearly related to the final shape as are those of later bifaces.

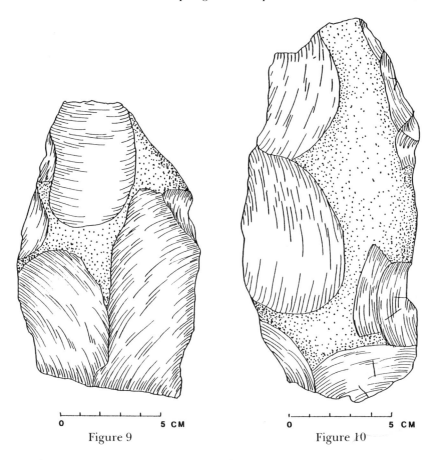

0 ⊢————————————⊣ 5 CM   0 ⊢————————————⊣ 5 CM
          Figure 9   Figure 10

Figure 10 (West Natron). This artifact is very similar to the previous one, but slightly more care was applied, especially to the right
margin. Again, it is not clear what any of the trimming flakes, taken
individually, has accomplished. For example, there is no obvious reason for the two scars at A, at least as far as the overall shape is
concerned.

These two bifaces from the early site of West Natron hold a transitional status not because of any clear-cut spatial patterns on the artifacts but because they cannot be accounted for with the competences
discussed for either the Oldowan or the later Acheulean. On the one
hand, a notion of order is not sophisticated enough for the creation
of the artifacts' overall shape. On the other hand, the haphazard placing of trimming argues against a competence in whole-part relations
as complete as those seen on the Isimila bifaces. The spatial competence of the West Natron hominids appears to have included some

notion of analysis and synthesis but one that was rather rudimentary.

The archaeological record does present, then, a developmental sequence of sorts in the ability to relate whole to parts. This competence required coordination of the spatial relations I discussed earlier, namely, proximity, separation, and order. Such coordination is the most sophisticated topological relation we can identify in stone artifacts. It is especially interesting that it is evident in artifacts of the Lower Palaeolithic.

One possible objection to the above discussion of whole-parts relations concerns the possible controlling factor of raw material. One could argue that the relative crudity of the West Natron bifaces was a consequence of poor raw material and that the Isimila artisans worked a more malleable type of stone, allowing liberties in planning and minimal trimming not available to their earlier counterparts. Recently Jones (1981) and Toth (1985) have made convincing arguments that raw material did, in fact, restrict the possible refinement of stone tools. But these results do not vitiate my argument concerning whole-part competences. First of all, the Isimila artisans used a fine-textured granite, not a particularly easy medium. More important, competence in whole-part relations is not a matter of crudity and fineness, nor even the amount of trimming, though the latter does help us recognize spatial abilities. From the perspective of crudity, example 7 is a relatively crude artifact; there are certainly much finer examples from Isimila. Whole-part competence is revealed in the way the knapper organizes his actions, and in this regard the minimum competence of the West Natron hominids was lower than that of the Isimila hominids.

Summary

Even though I have used the term "topological" to label the spatial concepts in this section, this use is at least a bit misleading. The nature of figures commonly identified with topology, such as Jordan curves, Klein bottles, and the bridges of Konigsberg, is not directly relevant to the question at hand. I am interested in the evolution of notions of space, and topological terms have allowed a more rigorous description of some of the simpler ones held by early hominids. These terms also supply a typology of increasingly complex spatial relations that has more explanatory power than such archaeological terms as "polyhedron" or "scraper." This typology can also be used to characterize developmental sequences.

Oldowan artifacts from Bed I at Olduvai required the spatial notions of *proximity, separation, the pair,* and *sequential order.* These spatial concepts were used by the hominids to control the placing of trimming blows on cobbles or, occasionally, on flakes. Some Oldowan artifacts required only that the cobble be bashed a number of times in the same general location. By simply striking two cobbles together repeatedly a hominid could achieve this. The spatial concept here, *proximity*, is very simple. The result is a tool with several projections and edges. If the hominid wanted to make a tool with a single edge, however, proximity alone would not suffice. He would need a concept of *separation*, in which the edge acts as a kind of boundary or reference separating faces of the tool. He would have to direct his blows with regard to that boundary; this concept is more complex than simple proximity. On many of the Oldowan artifacts, the knapper used a previous flake scar as a platform for the next. For this the knapper needed to conceive of each blow as an element to be placed in relation to another, and this required him to coordinate proximity and separation into a more specific spatial configuration—*the pair*. The Oldowan artifacts at Olduvai also include unifacially trimmed tools. In these cases, the idea of an edge once again required separation, but, beyond that, the knapper had to position the trimming blows in a rudimentary series in which sequential blows were spatially related to several preceding blows. This is a simple concept of *order*. All of these Oldowan concepts of space are simple, and, interestingly, all appear to be focused on the configuration of edges. There appear to have been no ideas about appropriate overall shape, nor any spatial concepts used solely to control overall shape.

It is possible to imagine simpler industries, and, indeed, there is some evidence for these. The tools from the two-million-year-old beds at Omo consist of smashed chunks of quartz and unmodified flakes (Merrick and Merrick 1976). The 1.8-million-year-old tools from East Turkana include choppers but lack the most spatially sophisticated Oldowan tools—the unifacial scrapers (Isaac 1976). On the surface, then, these artifacts are more spatially primitive than the tools from Bed I at Olduvai. However, given the smallness of both the Omo and the Turkana sample, I hesitate to attribute them to some kind of earlier "stage."

Notions of overall artifact shape appear after the Oldowan. Early biface assemblages like those from West Natron do not include the fine artifacts famous in later time periods; however, they do reveal some attention to overall shape. The knapper controlled his blows not just to produce edges but also to produce shapes, and this required spatial concepts of greater complexity than those of the Oldowan. One of these is an idea of the relation of parts to the whole, that is, how individual trimming blows work to achieve a desired shape. The West Natron hominids had some notion of this kind, but, given the crudity of their artifacts, it may have been only very rudimentary. Complicating the spatial picture of West Natron bifaces is the use of very large flakes as blanks. In most cases, however, the knapper appears to have further modified the overall shape of the flake; the blank's shape did not supply the overall shape of the tool. The West Natron hominids may also have had some notion of symmetry, which would require a reversal of shape—again, a relatively sophisticated concept. I will return to the symmetry argument later in the discussion of euclidean space.

The minimally trimmed bifaces from Isimila represent the most sophisticated concepts of topological space. Here the knapper directed blows to achieve an overall shape in a very economical manner. His spatial conception was much more complex than the Oldowan hominids' concept of a single edge. The Isimila hominid had to coordinate the notions of proximity and separation with a sophisticated idea of the relation of parts to the whole.

The Evidence for Projective Concepts

The preceding section dealt mostly with intuitively simple spatial concepts: nearness, separation, order, and so on. Even though simple, these notions were capable of producing effective working edges on stone. Indeed, many stone tools produced by historically known peoples required no more sophisticated spatial concepts than the topological notions used to manufacture Oldowan tools. But the patterns produced by such simple notions do not exhaust the stone-knapping repertoire of prehistoric hominids. Many stone tools exhibit patterns that suggest more sophisticated concepts of space. In this section and in the one following, I will examine these patterns and the spatial concepts they require. A review of evidence for projective concepts follows.

Projective geometry is a geometry of viewpoints or perspectives. It is concerned with qualities of figures that remain constant when the source of a projection changes. A simple way to explore projective relations is to study changes in shadows cast by a point source such as a candle or flashlight. One can easily transform the shadow of a square piece of cardboard into a rhombus or a trapezoid, but it is impossible to change the shadow into a triangle or a circle. Some qualities of the figure remain constant regardless of its relation to the light source. For example, straight lines are retained but angles and parallels change. "In projective geometry figures are equivalent if there is a projection carrying one onto another" (Chinn and Steenrud 1966:58). It is not only a geometry of shadows; it is also a geometry of viewpoints. The appearance of an object changes as the point of view of an observer changes, in the same manner as projections change. What is crucial is the orientation of the object and the observer to one another. This is a spatial relation that is external to the object itself. The topological relations discussed above remain constant regardless of perspective; they organize elements on a tool without any consideration of space beyond the boundaries of the tool itself. With projective relationships, spatial considerations external to the object are used to control aspects of its shape. In topology, as we have seen, rigidity of figures is irrelevant and figures such as squares, triangles, and circles are all equivalent. Projective geometry is more restrictive in its definition of equivalency. Nevertheless, it is like topology in that measurement—amount of space—is irrelevant. The size of an angle or a side or a curve is not a projective notion.

As was the case with topology, the axioms and theorems of projective geometry can be intimidating, but fortunately, as with topology, these formalizations are peripheral to our problem. We are interested in intuitive notions of space and, in particular, in how these intuitive notions govern the manufacture of stone tools. The intuitive notion of perspective is therefore of some interest. Do any patterns displayed by stone tools require concepts that include some consideration of perspective, that is, that consider the relative orientation of object and observer? At first this may appear unlikely, since the archaeological record does not preserve the relative position of knapper and artifact. Some archaeological sites do preserve relations of objects to one another—Stonehenge is an excellent example—but in the early Stone Age these are extremely rare and, like the stone circle at the Olduvai DK locality, not very informative in regard to perspective. We are left again with patterns internal to stone tools, and only a few of these suggest specific projective notions. The most notable are intentional straight edges and regular cross sections.

The projective straight line is no more than a topological line segment related to a stable viewpoint. All line segments are topologically equivalent because they respect relations of proximity, order, enclosure, and continuity. For every point on a curved line segment there is a corresponding point on a straight line segment. The line segments are equivalent because only relations internal to the figures are relevant. When the position of the observer is taken into account, certain spatial qualities are added to the simpler topological ones. A straight line viewed from the proper position becomes a point (the terminal point of a straight line is capable of masking all of the other points), but there is no position from which a curved line can be seen as a point. The ability to create a straight line presupposes an awareness of this stable viewpoint, either by actual sighting or by imagination. Alternatively, a straight line can be defined in euclidean terms of measurement and coordinate axes. As this is more complicated conceptually, it seems unlikely to have preceded projective notions of straightness.

What is true of projective straight lines must also be true of straight aspects of artifacts, but only if the straightness is clearly the result of intentional modification. This "if" is very restrictive. Straight edges are fairly common on Stone Age artifacts, yet those that are convincingly non-fortuitous are scarce. It is tempting, for example, to consider some cleaver bits to be intentionally straight. They are, after all, reminiscent of modern tools whose edges are usually straight. There are two reasons, though, for not considering the straightness of most cleaver bits to be deliberate. The first is that most bits are not really straight; curved and irregular, yes, but rarely straight. The second, and more important, is that cleavers were not, as a rule, manufactured with direct attention to the bit. The trimming and attention to shape were applied everywhere but to the bit, which remained a natural edge. The shape of this edge is not demonstrably intentional. It is therefore wrong to assume that any straightness of the bit reflects conceptual competence on the part of its maker. It could easily have been fortuitous. Much that is straight on stone tools is a result of manufacture on flakes, many of whose natural edges approach straightness. In order for one to argue about a competence in straight lines, the edge in question must be modified, and this modification must have considerably altered the natural shape of the edge.

Figure 11 (Isimila, sands 1). The trimmed lateral edge of this cleaver is remarkably straight, and, more important, the extent of the trimming suggests that the original shape of the edge was considerably altered. The edge is also straight in profile. This required the knapper to control two viewpoints or perspectives at the same time. Competence in the basic topological notions discussed in the previous chapter would not have been sufficient. The knapper had to have related the trimming of the edge to a constant point of view. Moreover, because the edge is also straight in profile, the knapper had to have considered a point of view located on another plane. Even if the knapper continually checked the edge by actual sighting, he had to be aware that the shape *varied according to the viewpoint*, that what was straight from one sighting point was perhaps not straight from another. In other words, some notion of perspective must have been present in the knapper's spatial repertoire, and a fairly sophisticated one at that since there are two coordinated perspectives evident here.

Because it is difficult to discount fortuitous straightness, document-

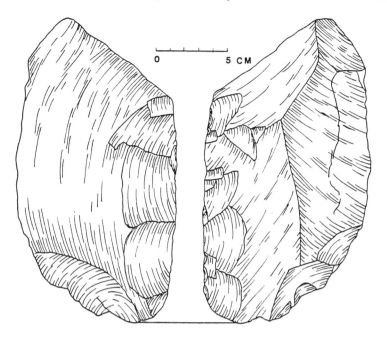

0   5 CM

Figure 11

ing rudimentary competence in a spatial notion of straightness presents a problem. Indeed it may be impossible. Nevertheless, I am going to describe one early Acheulean biface, not because it makes a convincing case, but rather because it illustrates the enigmatic nature of early Acheulean spatial notions.

Figure 12 (West Natron). The trimming on this artifact is much less extensive than that on example 11. Nevertheless, there is a certain straightness about the edges that seems unrelated to the shape of the original flake edge. This is especially true of the edge that was bifacially trimmed. The profile of this edge is not straight, however; indeed it is as sinuous as that of a chopper. I think it fair to conclude that there was some intent to modify the shape of the original flake. The spatial idea behind this modification *may* have included some adherence to perspective. But the straightness may also have been fortuitous. This example underlines the difficulty in evaluating projective geometry on the basis of stone tools. The medium itself causes difficulties. Documenting straightness requires extensive trimming and fine control. Not all raw materials are cooperative, and, moreover, we cannot expect that all knappers possessed the necessary motor skill. Stone knapping often produces more or less straight edges by chance, and, unless there is convincing evidence to the contrary, as in

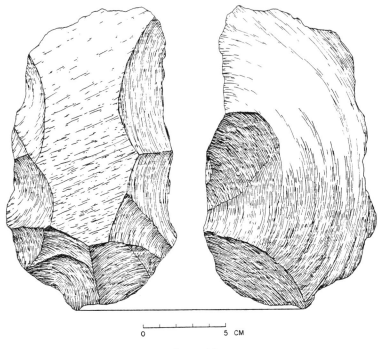

0   5 CM

Figure 12

example 11, we must be conservative and conclude that straightness was not intended.

As is true of the topological concept of analysis and synthesis, there is good evidence for consideration of perspective in later Acheulean bifaces. This competence included not only the ability to operate from one stable viewpoint but the ability to coordinate viewpoints. This conclusion is corroborated by the evidence from cross sections.

The cross section of an object is the two-dimensional shape produced by a plane intersecting the solid. For example, the cross section of a sphere is a circle; of a cylinder, a circle or an ellipse; of a pyramid, a rectangle. The cross section of a biface is the two-dimensional shape produced by an imaginary plane intersecting the artifact. We say that a biface has a "regular" cross section if it presents a recognizable two-dimensional figure such as a rhombus or a triangle or a lens shape. Symmetry is usually the most telling quality of regularity.

The ability to conceive of and create a regular cross section requires a sophisticated coordination of viewpoints or perspectives. First, it is necessary that the observer—in our case the knapper—be aware of a viewpoint that is not actually available to him. One cannot sight into a solid. Without the aid of some assisting apparatus such as a template, the image of the cross section must be imagined. Second, the observer must coordinate a virtual infinity of cross sections or perspectives. In a regular solid, a cylinder for example, all of the possible planar intersections will yield a two-dimensional cross section that is also regular. Almost none of these cross sections can be directly observed. The regularity aspects are a matter of euclidean notions, and will concern us in the next chapter. What is important here is that the perspective requirements, the coordination of viewpoints, are quite stringent in the matter of cross sections.

As with the projective straight line, the medium of stone places certain limits on the study of cross sections. Very fine cross sections are easy to recognize; it is the cruder cross sections that present difficulties. For example, large flakes often have a "natural" cross section that is fairly regular without any modification by the knapper. It again becomes necessary to emphasize extensively trimmed artifacts, a procedure that risks underestimating the competence of a stone knapper who simply took advantage of a natural bonus.

Figure 13 (Isimila, sands 1). The first cross section is that of a very fine biface from Isimila. The cross section was taken with a template at the point of maximum width. As can be seen from Figure 13, the artifact is extensively trimmed, and it is fair to conclude that the original shape of the blank, including the cross section, has been changed. Could the knapper have controlled the shape of this cross section by directly sighting from a perspective to the rear of the artifact? Such a direct sighting would actually combine (and confound) the dimensions of maximum width and maximum thickness, which do not fall at the same point on the length of the artifact (maximum thickness is farther toward the tip). In other words, the knapper would see a "view" that was a composite of two separate cross sections. There is, in fact, no position from which the cross section of the artifact in Figure 13 can be directly observed. It must be created in the imagination or, as I have done, measured with a device. Moreover, a planar intersection taken virtually anywhere on this artifact, even at angles not parallel to the major axes, would yield a regular cross section. The knapper constructed not just one imaginary viewpoint but a virtual infinity of them. His control in this regard was quite remarkable.

Figures 14 and 15 (Isimila). The three cross sections figured here are also of Isimila bifaces. Cross sections 14a and 14b are from the minimally trimmed bifaces in Figures 7 and 8. Neither is an especially fine piece. The cross section of 14a is regular, but this regularity is spurious; the minimal trimming used by the knapper did little to alter the natural cross section of the flake blank. In order to accept a cross

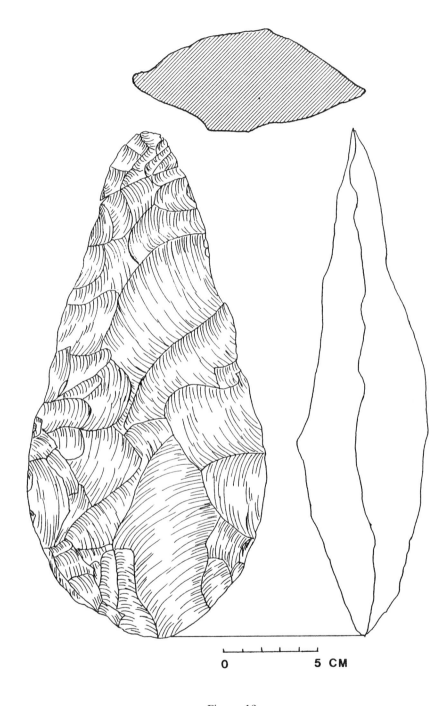

0   5 CM

Figure 13

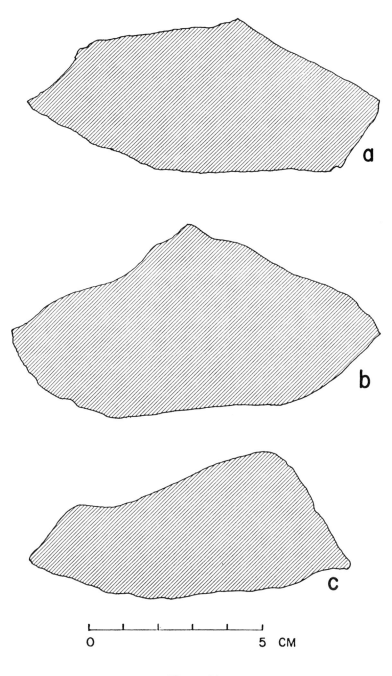

O   5   CM

Figure 14

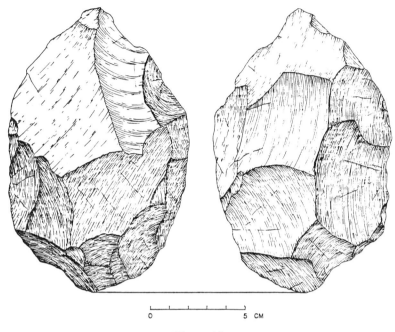

0   5 CM

Figure 15

section as intentional, it is necessary that the artifact be extensively modified. (Neither 14a nor 14b qualifies despite the vague regularity of the cross section itself.) But not all extensively trimmed bifaces have a regular cross section. 14c is the cross section of the biface in Figure 15. Even though the knapper trimmed the piece rather extensively, the cross section is irregular, almost as if the knapper had not attended to it at all. These examples are cautionary and I include them to emphasize the care that must be taken in determining the necessary competence of hominid stone knappers. Regularity in stone tools can be accidental, and, moreover, even extensively trimmed artifacts can be irregular. But the knapper of example 13 must have considered the cross section. If he had not, the result would have been like that for examples 14c and 15.

The fine bifaces from late sites such as Isimila all have regular cross sections. However, such artifacts are by no means the most common. Almost all biface assemblages, even very late ones, have crude bifaces with irregular cross sections. In many assemblages these predominate. Nevertheless, in a study such as this one, which is concerned with the evolution of a competence, it is fair, I think, to focus on the exceptional pieces. The crudest obviously do not represent the most sophisticated competence of a particular period. The examples that follow, then, are also of the finest artifacts from their respective collections.

Figures 16 and 17 (West Natron). Both of these bifaces are from the RHS locality at West Natron. Neither artifact's cross section shows the symmetrical regularity occasionally seen on the Isimila bifaces. However, the *plan* shape of each of these artifacts is at least roughly symmetrical. I will treat the symmetry later; what is important here is that there is attention to regularity in plan, which can be directly checked, but no clear attention to cross section, which would have required imaginary perspectives. The cross section of example 16 is very vaguely symmetrical, but if we examine the trimming patterns, it is clear that this regularity may have been fortuitous. One face of the original flake has been little altered and the trimming on the opposite face presents little in the way of a coherent pattern (see earlier discussion of whole-parts relations). Example 17 also presents a rough bilateral symmetry, but has very little trimming. The result is an irregular cross section. We are encountering here the same problem we confronted with the evidence for straight lines. Unless the artifact is extensively trimmed and extremely regular, it is difficult, if not impossible, to document projective relations. The minimum necessary competence does not, therefore, include projective notions.

Figures 18 and 19 (West Natron). The four cross sections in Figure 18 are from MHS locality bifaces. Example 18a at first glance appears regular, but examination of Figure 19 indicates that once again this regularity is fortuitous. Yet 18a is the "best" cross section that the MHS locality has to offer. It is impossible to conclude that there was any attention paid to the shape of these artifacts' cross sections, at least any attention requiring an imaginary perspective.

Evidence for intentional regular cross sections among the earlier Oldowan artifacts is nonexistent. One could perhaps argue that the so-called spheroids and discoids from Bed I Olduvai sites have, as their names imply, regular cross sections. However, without exception, the cross sections of these artifacts are irregular, and there is no basis for arguing for a *notion* of cross section. I will return to these artifacts later in this study, for they are informative in regard to other aspects of spatial competence.

As was the case with the projective straight line, the developmental sequence of the notion of regular cross section is far from complete. The bifaces from Isimila are more sophisticated than the earlier bifaces from West Natron. Many of the former exhibit regular, symmetrical cross sections while none of the latter do. Moreover, the fine cross sections of the Isimila bifaces resulted from extensive bifacial trimming that also produced symmetry in plan and profile. The trim-

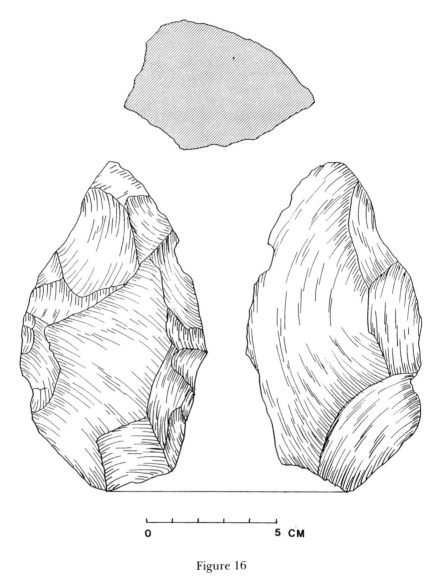

0   5 CM

Figure 16

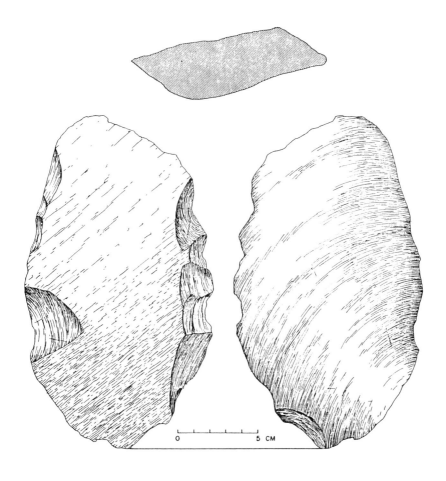

Figure 17

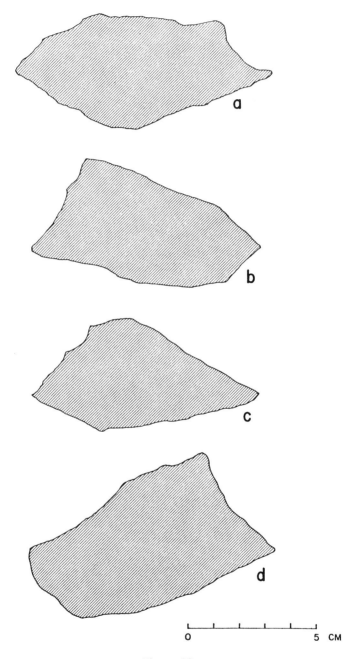

0   5 CM

Figure 18

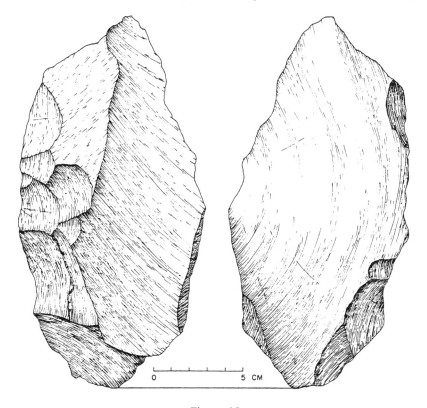

0 | | | | | | 5 CM

Figure 19

ming on the West Natron bifaces, on the other hand, produced no more than a rudimentary bilateral symmetry. Without extensive trimming it is difficult to argue for any kind of intention. Some of the West Natron bifaces, such as example 16, are extensively trimmed but lack regular cross sections. Without any examples to the contrary, we must accept these as the best the West Natron hominids were capable of producing. We can conclude, tentatively at least, that the Isimila hominids were able to control stone knapping by using viewpoints that were not actually available to them and that had to be imagined. Furthermore, they had to consider many such viewpoints simultaneously. The West Natron hominids apparently did not possess this spatial ability. It is, of course, unlikely that this ability appeared full-blown one day; it must have evolved. Unfortunately, a satisfactory sequence does not exist at present, and, indeed, it is hard to think what a transitional form might look like. We again run afoul of the medium. It seems likely, for example, that competence in a few of the more accessible cross sections would have been a first step. But could we discern this concept in patterns on the tool? Perhaps, and perhaps not. We can hope to resolve the problem with assemblages that fall chronologically between West Natron and Isimila, but as it now stands, our sequence is not much of one. Isimila hominids used the concept of the cross section; West Natron hominids did not.

Summary

The ability to distinguish and coordinate independent perspectives is an important component of modern adult concepts of space. It is commonplace for us to imagine how an object or scene will appear from another perspective (we even use similar skills to measure intelligence on standard tests). It is an efficient and useful way to apprehend the world. Without this ability, the world would constantly present unfamiliar scenes. Even well-known objects would, if approached or seen from a new angle, appear different because of the inability to imagine how they would appear from the other, familiar angle. Young children do not possess this concept, and its absence yields an interesting notion of space. For example, when presented objects arranged into a scene, young children consider the relative spatial position to be permanent; that is, they assume that the left-right and front-back order that is visible from their perspective is the same for all other observers. When asked to predict the shape of a shadow on a screen, they describe the object as they see it from their own position. In other words, young children do not consider viewpoints other than their own (Piaget and Inhelder 1967). Seen in this light, projective notions become more than just amusing shadow games and unfamiliar geometric axioms. They are important spatial notions. Awareness of independent points of view implies that an individual recognizes that both he and the object exist within a space of changing relative positions.

It is clear from the artifacts discussed above that the Isimila hominids were capable of imagining and coordinating independent points of view and of placing themselves within a space of changing relations. Their mastery of cross section and their notion of straight edges both attest to this ability. Given the topological sophistication of these artifacts, this conclusion is not surprising. Indeed, the topological and projective geometry of the Isimila artifacts corroborate one another. What is not clear is the development of these projective abilities. No argument can be made for projective relations during the Oldowan. No straight edges exist, and there are no intentionally regular cross sections. The West Natron artifacts are more equivocal. Some are extensively trimmed, some have vaguely straight sides, and some of the bifaces have somewhat regular cross sections. Unfortunately, however, we cannot argue that the regularity of these cross sections was intentional because the original cross section of the blank is not seriously altered; the regularity could be fortuitous. In other words, the "intermediate" position of West Natron artifacts in regard to topological relations is not corroborated by their position in regard to projective relations. These appear to have been a relatively late addition to the hominid repertoire.

The Evidence for Euclidean Concepts

In the section on topology, I discussed fundamental spatial notions applied to stone knapping. All dealt with relations internal to the artifacts. In the section on projective space, I examined how consideration of perspective, an external relation in space, affects the shape of artifacts. But projective relations still consider only a specific relationship between the viewer and the object. In this chapter, I will discuss the development of general constructions of space, spatial notions that transcend individual objects and their relations and organize space into a framework in which objects occupy positions.

A euclidean space is one of positions, not of objects. It is defined by an arbitrary framework, a set of coordinates, for example. In a sense, one empties space of objects and organizes what is left by means of a reference system that consists of all of the potential positions objects may hold. Such a space requires intervals, which are units of consistent spatial *quantity*. Amount of space is irrelevant to topological and projective space, but it is one of the key concepts around which euclidean space is built. Spatial intervals act as an independent and constant reference against which objects can be compared and located in space.

A space of positions is the space in which modern adults habitually act and think. Whether or not it is consciously thought of as a three-dimensional coordinate grid, the everyday world (the life-world of phenomenologists) is acted upon as if space were a given and immutable entity in which objects occupied positions. However, ". . . it would be a complete mistake to imagine that human beings have some innate or psychologically precocious knowledge of the spatial surround organized in a two- or three-dimensional reference frame" (Piaget and Inhelder 1967:416). The idea of space as a general framework of positions is one that develops during ontogeny, and, as I hope to show in this section, it appeared in the behavior of early humans by 300,000 years ago.

The idea of a euclidean coordinate space incorporates two simpler spatial notions, that of measurement and that of parallel axes. Be-

cause it is unlikely that a concept of euclidean space sprang fully developed out of the head of some *Homo erectus* Zeus, I am first going
to explore the evidence for these simpler notions, on the assumption
that they should appear first. As it turns out, there is early evidence
for a concept of measurement but not for one of parallel axes, a fact
that has interesting implications for the evolution of euclidean space.

By a concept of measurement, I mean any notion of a relatively
constant amount of space used as a reference of some sort. This need
not be a formally defined idea of meters or inches, but could be
such readily available references as hand breadth and literal feet. Of
course, it would be difficult to document the use of such intervals in
prehistory. However, there are two constant intervals that appear to
have been used fairly early in the manufacture of some stone tools—
the radius and diameter. When a line segment is rotated around one
of its terminal points, the result is a circle. One can actually perform
this simple feat with a string or even a stick. To make a circle in stone
one cannot rotate a physical radius, but must use a *concept* of radius
or diameter as a constant length against which the artifact is compared. The interval of a radius is not general, but is specific to a
particular tool. Nevertheless, it is an interval that consists, however
briefly, of a constant quantity of space.

Figure 20 (upper Bed II, Olduvai). This is an excellent example of
a discoid. Discoid is a label used by archaeologists for artifacts, usually
bifacially trimmed, that are more or less round in plan. The reference
is to the artifact's two-dimensional shape. The cross section is irrelevant. The amount of trimming on this discoid suggests that the final
shape was probably intentional. The rudimentary spatial notions of
order and separation are insufficient to explain this artifact; the knapper must have employed some additional spatial concept. At the minimum, he must have used some concept of radius or diameter, that is,

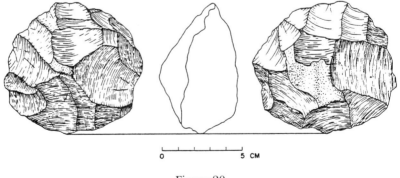

Figure 20

some notion of a constant amount of space separating all of the edges. Alternatively, he might have used some idea of a regular curve, employing a reference system of chords and arcs. But this is even more complex than a radius. We may conclude that the knapper of this discoid used some notion of interval, either radius or diameter, while making this artifact. Again, I do not mean to argue that the knapper was a geometrician and reflected upon such concepts, only that he used a simple notion of interval in his spatial repertoire.

Figure 21. These artifacts are more equivocal, though still typed as discoids. Artifacts a and b are from Bed I at Olduvai and so are equivalent in age to the choppers and scrapers discussed in the chapter on topology. I find it impossible to argue for a notion of radius or diameter here. The circumferences are quite irregular, at least compared to the one in example 20, and the knapper appears to have made little effort to equalize the diameters by knocking off projections (a) or by "pulling in" edges (b). Moreover, neither artifact is extensively trimmed, making it hard to argue for an intentional shape. In both cases, the minimum necessary competence is the same as that for the choppers discussed earlier—a notion of separation, pairs, and perhaps order. The difference between these artifacts and choppers of the same age is that here, more of the circumference of a cobble has been trimmed. The disc shape is probably fortuitous.

Example 21c is more circular in appearance than either a or b, and indeed in one perspective (the left) is even more circular than example 20. It is the amount of trimming that makes me cautious; the shape just might be fortuitous. Interestingly, the artifact comes from HWK East level 4, the one HWK East level that dates to *upper* Bed II, the same general stratigraphic position as that of the discoid in Figure 20.

In sum, the discoids from upper Bed II at Olduvai argue for some notion of radius or diameter, that is, a relatively constant amount of space used as a reference. Many of the Olduvai localities have also yielded roughly spherical artifacts, sometimes called "stone balls." While typologically all may qualify as spheroids, they do not all require the same spatial concepts.

Plates 1 and 2 (Olduvai Gorge, various levels). I have arranged these four artifacts in stratigraphic order for comparative purposes. Mary Leakey has typed all as spheroids. The "evolution" of the shape is a bit misleading. There is no smooth progression of artifacts; each is the "best" from its respective assemblage. The artifact in plate 2 is the best from all of the Olduvai assemblages, and, indeed, is one of the most spherical spheroids I have ever seen. It truly deserves the name "stone ball."

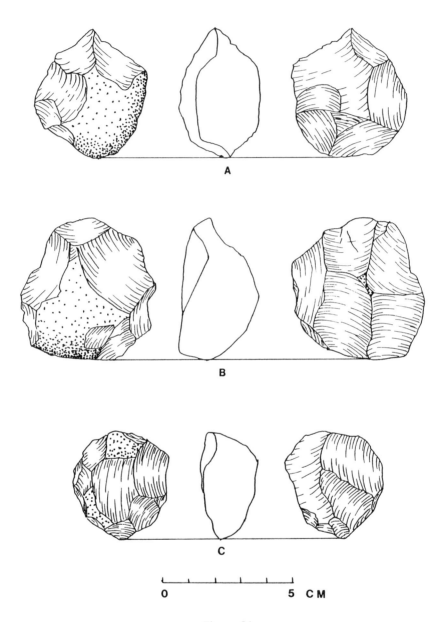

A

B

C

0   5 CM

Figure 21

A

B

C

Plate 1

Plate 2

Is it possible that spheroids resulted not from some spatial concept of interval but simply from the copying of a model in nature—a fruit, for example? This is a knotty problem to which I will return later in the discussion of symmetry. At this point, we can gain some insight by looking at copying in drawing. When young children are asked to copy euclidean forms, they are successful only after they have developed an understanding of euclidean space (Piaget and Inhelder 1967). Very young children copy only the topological attributes of the figures. It appears, then, that attempts to copy natural spheres in stone would be successful only if the knapper understood the basic geometric concept of radial symmetry. Prior to this the spheroids would respect only topological notions. Furthermore, though this is a minor point, a perfect copy of an apple would not be a sphere. It just seems highly unlikely that the spheroid in plate 2 is a copy of anything.

If they are not copies, these fine spheroids must reflect the use of some spatial notion, and the minimum spatial notion is that of the interval, in this case a constant diameter. As with the discoids, this interval need not have been a general, abstract measurement, but simply a continuous reference to one original interval inherent in the artifact. Nevertheless, this is a constant *quantity* of space. The spheroid in plate 2 certainly argues for such a notion, as does, I believe, the spheroid in plate 1c. It seems highly unlikely that either's regularity is fortuitous. The artifacts in plates 1a and 1b are another matter. Their shapes are only roughly spherical and could easily be fortuitous; indeed, from the perspective of minimum necessary competence, they are no more than extensively trimmed polyhedrons. Perhaps they are, in fact, crude copies of natural objects. They are what we would expect from a basic topological competence. They could well have been produced using only a concept of proximity; the knapper might simply have struck the artifact again and again, placing blows near one another, until he attained his desired result. However, we are in no position to speculate about motivation; we do not even know if the shape was intentional.

In sum, the evidence from the spheroids corroborates that of the discoids. On the one hand, the shape regularities of the earlier Bed I artifacts require only a competence in order, the placing of trimming blows in some relation to previous blows. Trimming the complete circumference of a flake or cobble could easily produce a vague disc or sphere without any intention on the part of the hominid knapper to do so. On the other hand, the regularity and the amount of trimming on the upper Bed II spheroids and discoids represent some additional spatial concept, in this case a concept of interval.

I do not wish to overemphasize the importance of a concept of interval. It is not in and of itself evidence for a competence in euclidean space. However, the notion of a quantity of space is one of the prerequisites to euclidean concepts, and here we have it, in rudimentary form perhaps, in the regular diameters of upper Bed II discoids and spheroids.

A second spatial notion that is an element of euclidean space is that of parallel axes, which are essential to the formal definition of a coordinate grid. Actually, parallels constitute a geometry all their own, termed "affine" geometry, with its own set of axioms and theorems. While it is possible to define parallel lines using euclidean notions of angles and measurement, it is not necessary to do so. Any two lines on a plane that never meet are parallel. This definition assumes a concept of plane, but in practice is well within the competence of an intuitive geometry. This does not mean, however, that it *must* exist as an independent notion in an intuitive conception of space, nor that it must precede a truly euclidean geometry in a developmental sequence. It would, of course, be nice and tidy if it did.

The same caveats hold when one examines stone tools for parallel edges that hold when one inspects them for projective relations. It is especially hard to prove intention.

Figure 22 (Isimila). The lateral edges of this cleaver are extensively trimmed, and it is fair to assume that the overall shape was intentional. The parallel here is about as good as one could hope to achieve by bifacial trimming. This artifact actually approaches being a regular quadrilateral. But does it exemplify a notion of parallel, or is the parallel just a side effect of bilateral symmetry, which is not an affine concept?

0   5   CM

Figure 22

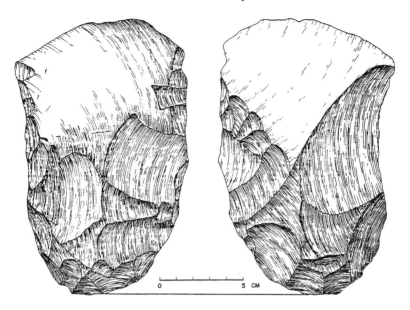

0   5 CM

Figure 23

Figure 23 (Isimila). This cleaver's lateral edges are at least roughly parallel; however, the tool is not bilaterally symmetrical. Here the parallel could not, therefore, be an effect of bilateral symmetry. This is not a unique artifact. There are several other Isimila cleavers with this attractive curved parallel pattern.

Figure 24 (Isimila). This cleaver also has roughly parallel lateral edges, though here intention is harder to accept because of the minimal amount of trimming. Nevertheless, this minimal trimming is suggestive because it argues for an idea of shape, and for an efficient plan for achieving it.

Based on artifacts such as these, an argument could be made that the Isimila hominids had some concept of parallel in their spatial repertoire. However, there need not have been a concept of parallel that was separate from euclidean notions of space since, as we shall see, there are euclidean notions such as congruency that were used by the Isimila hominids. To document a separate use of affine spatial relations, we would need an assemblage in which affine but not euclidean relations were required. To my knowledge no such assemblage exists. In neither the West Natron assemblages nor the Olduvai Bed I and Bed II assemblages are there artifacts that have parallel edges. Competence in parallels appeared at the same time as competence in euclidean space. As a consequence, one cannot argue for the existence

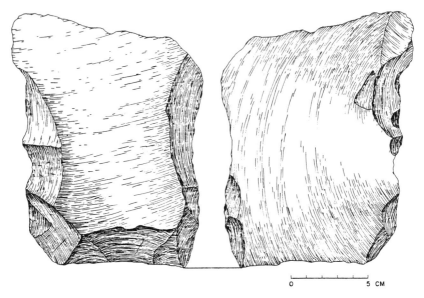

Figure 24

of affine relations as separate from euclidean ones at any point in the phylogeny of spatial competence.

This argument about affine geometry may appear, I admit, rather like sophistry. But it does bear on two important aspects of our problem—the antecedents of euclidean concepts and the relation between developmental and "logical" sequences. The lack of an affine "stage" will turn out to be quite important.

Rectilinear and Curvilinear Shapes

Before considering bilateral symmetry, I need to discuss a topic that is not strictly topological, projective, or euclidean but that does bear on the development of spatial competence. This is the distinction between rectilinear and curvilinear shapes, especially in regard to the shapes of artifact edges.

Figure 25 a-c (Olduvai upper Bed II). Mary Leakey typed all of these artifacts as "awls," presumably because of the trimmed projection present on each. The position of the trimming on each artifact does suggest that these projections were, in fact, intentional. What (if anything) does this intention reveal about the knapper's spatial repertoire? It indicates that he distinguished, at a minimum, between smooth curves and "pointy" shapes, and that he preferred one over the other in certain circumstances. Once again we have a rather sim-

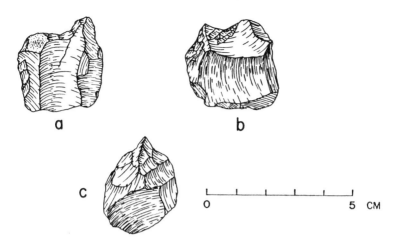

a   b

c   0   5 CM

Figure 25

ple notion that is in itself not surprising. And once again, analogy to child development gives us a starting point for interpretation.

When children are asked to copy geometric figures, their first efforts consist of drawing simple closed figures for all closed shapes—squares, circles, triangles, and so on, are not differentiated. The first advance over these "topological" efforts is the distinguishing of rectilinear shapes from curvilinear ones (Piaget and Inhelder 1967). The child makes the distinction not by drawing straight lines (a sophisticated idea, as we have seen) but by intersecting lines into angles. He discriminates between sharp pointed and smoothly curved shapes. In physical terms, this requires the interruption and coordination of the rhythmic motor patterns of drawing and, in the case of awls, stone knapping. An awl differs from a scraper only in that the shape of the latter is a fairly even curve while that of the former is interrupted by a point. This is a simple kind of shape discrimination, and yet is among the earliest we can recognize in both ontogeny and the archaeological record.*

Bilateral Symmetry

Bilateral symmetry in its strict sense is a euclidean concept. "Two points are said to be *symmetrical with respect to a point,* P, if P bisects

---

*Leakey (1971) mentions the presence of an awl at the Bed I site of DK. I was unable to find this artifact, as much of the DK material was not in Nairobi at the time of my analysis. I do not doubt its existence.

the line segment joining the two points. . . . Two figures can be considered symmetrical with respect to a point (line) if each point in one figure has a symmetrical point in the other drawing" (Konkle 1974:94, emphasis in original). In the case of symmetry with respect to a line (bilateral symmetry), the bisecting line must be perpendicular to the segment joining any two symmetrical points. The notions of "bisect" and "perpendicular" require the quantitative concepts of angle and distance (concepts of rotational and linear measurement). A simpler intuitive notion of symmetry consists of mirror images, one an exact but reversed duplicate of the other. Yet even here the idea of an exact duplicate usually means a congruency, which is of course a euclidean notion requiring conserved amounts of space and angle.

In this section I will examine the development of bilateral symmetry by citing examples of artifacts that required a reversal about a perpendicular bisecting line (which I will simply term a midline) as well as some notion of symmetrical congruency, that is, the theoretical infinity of symmetrical points that constitute symmetrical figures.

Symmetry is a quality that one can easily—perhaps too easily—perceive in artifacts. Symmetry is so much a part of the everyday world, especially that of Western culture, that it is second nature to see it where it does not really exist. It is a kind of "good Gestalt." The human face is an excellent example. There are corresponding points on each side—eyes, ears, nostrils, and so on—but they are rarely, if ever, in true symmetry to one another. One ear is lower, or the nose is crooked. We see faces as true symmetries because we have a concept of symmetry; we certainly do not simply perceive it. If symmetry were an idea that was simply generalized from perceptions of the natural world, then children should possess an idea of symmetry at a fairly early stage. Evidence from children's drawing, however, argues against this. Even after children have acquired the motor coordination for drawing, they do not draw symmetrical figures (Piaget and Inhelder 1967). They cannot even *copy* symmetries with any degree of accuracy. Children do not attend to the symmetries in drawings until they have achieved an understanding of euclidean relations. Once this has occurred, the concept of symmetry can be applied to perception, and figures can be recognized as symmetrical. Because this study is concerned with the conceptual abilities of early hominids, not of archaeologists, it is important to avoid a too-willing acceptance of an artifact as symmetrical. This does not mean that only metrically precise symmetries can be considered, but it does suggest that vaguely symmetrical artifacts may represent not a concept of symmetry on the part of the stone knapper, but a concept of symmetry on the part of the archaeologist.

   With that caution out of the way, we can examine some of the relevant artifacts.

   Once again consider the artifact in Figure 13, whose cross sections were used in the earlier discussion on projective space. I think it is obvious that whoever made this handaxe had some notion of symmetry. It is not only bilaterally symmetrical in plan, it is symmetrical in profile and in all of its cross sections. Furthermore it is extensively trimmed, and the shapes are certainly intentional. The symmetry is extremely regular, and the mirrored shapes are congruent. One could improve little on the result if one were to use a measuring device. The symmetries in this artifact come very close to fulfilling the formal definition of symmetry presented at the beginning of this section.

   An even more powerful argument for a concept of symmetry can be based on minimally trimmed artifacts.

   Figure 26 (Isimila). The trimming at A especially suggests attention to mirroring a congruent shape. The bit has been "pulled in" for the same distance on the retouched margin as it was naturally done on the opposite margin. The subsequent constriction extends for the

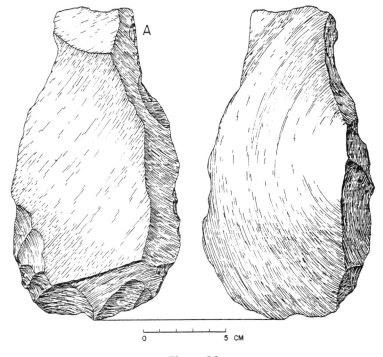

0   5 CM

Figure 26

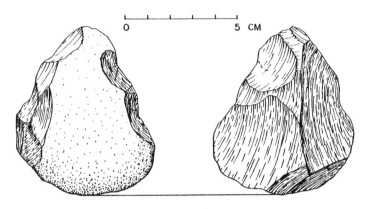

Figure 27

same length along each side. The knapper also trimmed the butt into an even curve, giving the artifact an excellent symmetry in plan with minimal effort. The biface discussed earlier in Figure 7 presents a similar approach to achieving symmetry. Both of these artifacts argue for a concept of the relation between whole and parts. They also suggest that the conceived "whole" was in large part defined by a concept of symmetry. In both cases, some notion of mirroring and of congruency of shape must have been part of the knapper's spatial repertoire.

The handaxe in Figure 13 also suggests something even more remarkable than simple bilateral symmetry. The artifact demonstrates symmetry across not just a midline in plan, but also a midline in profile and a midline for all of the cross sections. These lines intersect to define a three-dimensional space, intuitively equivalent to a space of Cartesian coordinates. It is difficult to imagine how a more sophisticated conception of space could be employed in stone knapping. Artifacts like this one constitute the endpoint of our developmental sequence.

The beginning point of the development of bilateral symmetry is much harder to identify.

Figure 27 (Olduvai lower Bed II). Mary Leakey has typed this artifact as a proto-biface, a term that has at least some implications for symmetries since most bifaces, that in Figure 13 for example, are symmetrical. The artifact does have bifacial trimming, but this in itself is not enough to distinguish it from artifacts like choppers and discoids. The defining criterion seems to lie in the shape, which, at first glance, does resemble a bilateral symmetry. However, there is nothing about the location of trimming that suggests that the shape of the original cobble was significantly altered. The greater amount of trimming on the left margin may have been placed to "pull in" that edge, but such

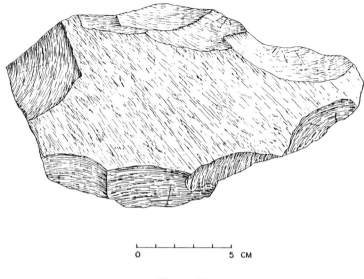

0   5 CM

Figure 28

a conclusion is pure speculation. There is no good reason to conclude that there was any notion of mirroring or congruency in the spatial repertoire of this stone knapper. In this case, the symmetry is in the heads of the archaeologists.

Figure 28 (West Natron). The question of symmetry for this artifact is made more difficult by the nature of the blank, a large flake. The lateral edges are, roughly, mirror images of one another. The trimming, while fairly continuous, is not extensive, and it is therefore impossible to know with any certainty that the original shape of the blank has been altered. The relatively continuous trimming of large flakes will, I imagine, often result in vaguely symmetrical artifacts. But such symmetry is a by-product of the shape of the blank and is not demonstrably intentional. The bifaces in Figures 9 and 10 are more typical of the West Natron bifaces. They have comparable amounts of trimming, but few archaeologists would argue for bilateral symmetry.

Figure 29 (Olduvai upper Bed II). I include this example because it is from the earliest dated Acheulean site at Olduvai, and also because it resembles, superficially, the much later Isimila artifact in Figure 26. The difference lies in the amount of trimming. The extensive trimming on the Figure 26 biface argues for a notion of symmetry because it allows us to conclude that the shape was intended. But here the single large trimming blow near the bit is not sufficient to allow a similar conclusion. Nevertheless, the similarity between the two is pro-

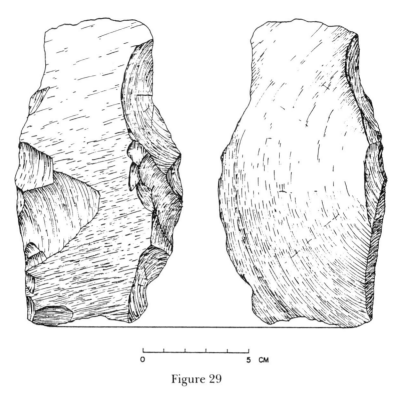

0   5 CM

Figure 29

vocative. The symmetry of this artifact is more difficult to discount than that of the West Natron bifaces.

Figure 30 (Olduvai upper Bed II). The symmetry of this biface is even more difficult to refute. It is similar in age to the previous example. The shape of the right lateral edge is mirrored on the left. Moreover, the artifact is extensively trimmed, and the overall shape is unlikely to correspond to the shape of the blank (in this case a core, not a flake). There appears to have been some notion of mirroring. Whether or not this notion is equivalent to the euclidean concepts seen later among Isimila bifaces is an important matter of interpretation for documenting the development of spatial concepts. I intend to show that it is not necessarily equivalent.

If we limit our consideration of symmetry to euclidean concepts of congruency, perpendicular and bisected lines, and so on, then the developmental sequence presented by stone tools consists of only two stages—early stone tools for which an argument for symmetry cannot be made, and later artifacts, like those from Isimila, for which it must be made. This is not much of a sequence, and, in fact, it tells us noth-

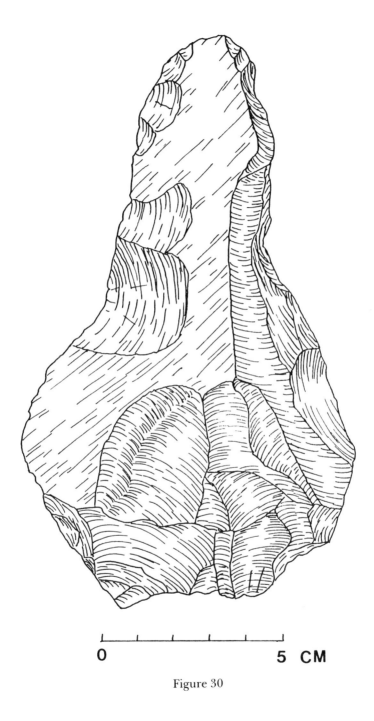

0   5 CM

Figure 30

ing about the antecedents of euclidean notions, which is just what we would like to know.

Even though we have defined symmetry using euclidean notions (primarily because this is relatively easy to do), there is also a more primitive spatial notion at work, the notion of reversal. Recall from the earlier discussion of topological concepts that symmetry requires a reversal of order. When the order that is reversed includes a notion of conserved amount of space, as appears the case with the Isimila bifaces, then we are dealing with a case of congruency. As we have seen, a notion of congruency is extremely doubtful for the bifaces from West Natron and upper Bed II at Olduvai. Yet a mirroring of some sort seems to be evident. What has been reversed if not a congruent shape? Certain internal relationships of the shapes have been conserved, though no accurately measured distances. The concept of geometrical similarity is of some use here. Two figures are similar if the internal angles are the same—size is irrelevant. In a strict sense, symmetrical similar figures would also be congruent because they would share one side. What is of use in the concept of similarity here is the notion of similar internal angles, which we can expand to include curves. As we saw in the previous section, notions of rectilinear and curved forms appear fairly early and do not require complex euclidean notions.

Such configurations can be duplicated by repeating the relative position of curves and angles, which is a kind of geometrical "similarity." For example, a rudimentary S is a simple recurve, a shape that is repeatable with no reference to amounts of space, just an internal relation of curves. It is also reversible.

If we combine such notions of shape with a notion of mirroring, that is, a reversal of order, we have a primitive kind of bilateral symmetry in the absence of any euclidean concepts.

The resulting sequence is more complete than the one using purely euclidean symmetry. The early Oldowan demonstrated a notion of rectilinear and curvilinear shapes in plan. The early bifaces from West Natron and Olduvai suggest that a notion of reversal or mirroring could be applied to similar curves, resulting in a primitive kind of bilateral symmetry. Finally, by the time of Isimila, a more precise form of symmetry employed notions such as conserved amounts of space and congruency.

Summary

A euclidean space is a space of positions, one that entails the spatial patterns within objects, the relative positions of objects, and, indeed, the *potential* (and unrealized) patterns within and of objects. As such, it is a general theory of space which modern humans find very useful. What can we conclude about its evolution? The artifacts themselves are not fossilized theories, but they do supply clues to the antecedents of such a general frame of reference.

The hominids who made the Isimila bifaces almost certainly employed a general spatial framework, intuitively equivalent to a space of euclidean coordinates. Direct evidence of a three-dimensional coordinate space made up of an infinity of possible positions is, of course, unavailable from artifacts. Nevertheless, competence in such a space appears likely. The fine bifaces, like those in example 13, have bilateral symmetry in three dimensions (as we would define them). The knapper had to be able to invert congruent shapes across an imaginary midline for three separate dimensions *and* to coordinate them. This required a frame of reference of considerable complexity, and, while I suppose it possible that this frame was applied only to spatial relations on or within artifacts, this seems to me very unlikely. The abstract nature of such a spatial framework suggests that it was a general one, extendable to all of space. Again I must emphasize that the knapper need not have been able to describe or to verbalize his concepts in nice mathematical terms. That he employed such a framework, however, is, I think, undeniable.

The development of this concept of space is harder to document. Interestingly, the evidence is not quite what one would expect from a strictly Piagetian perspective.

In Piaget and Inhelder's major work on the development of spatial concepts (Piaget and Inhelder 1967), they repeatedly emphasize that two notions precede the appearance of a euclidean-like reference system. One is the development of an understanding of parallels, and the other is the understanding of similarity or equivalent angles. They further argue that this sequence is identical to a sequence of formal mathematical complexity, that it is in some sense logically entailed. If it is a logically necessary sequence we should, of course, see it in the phylogenetic sequence as well. But this is not quite what we find.

There appears to have been no "affine" stage in which stone knappers had a competence in parallels but not in euclidean relations. All of the artifacts that present artificially parallel edges occur in assemblages that have bilateral symmetry with congruency in three dimensions. It is possible that this absence of a supposed necessary antecedent is a product of a less-than-ideal archaeological record. There are huge chronological gaps in our sequence of assemblages, so it is quite possible that we do not see important acquisitions until long after they occurred. However, we do know that certain other notions did appear earlier, and, indeed, seem to have been crucial antecedents to euclidean concepts.

The first is the concept of interval. I think it is evident from the discoids and spheroids from upper Bed II at Olduvai that the hominids there employed some notion of a constant radius or diameter. The shapes of some of these artifacts are just too regular to be fortuitous. The diameter was an amount of space against which the knapper compared his artifact. It was a "real" amount of space that the knapper could see more or less continuously. It does represent a step up in abstraction, but there is no reason to suppose that these intervals were abstracted beyond the artifact at hand. These spatial quantities were tied to specific artifacts; using one diameter as a reference for other intervals on the same artifact does not require an abstract notion of measurement. These seem to have been internal, actually tangible referents.

The second antecedent notion was of the two-dimensional shape. By this I mean simple curves, projections, concavities, and so on. The existence of tools like awls suggests that the hominids recognized certain two-dimensional shapes and made efforts to produce them. Again, this implies some frame of reference beyond the proximity and order of simple topological notions. It is, of course, not necessary to understand euclidean space to produce an awl; topological notions alone, however, are insufficient.

The third antecedent notion is reversal, in particular the mirroring of one shape across a midline. Some of the early bifaces almost certainly required the ability to mirror the shape of one lateral edge with its opposite. Once again this is not euclidean, but it does require some kind of internal frame allowing the knapper to conceive of the shape of the artifact as a whole.

These three spatial notions, taken singly or together, do not constitute a general theory of a space of positions. Indeed, none appears to have been applied beyond what could be directly perceived by the knapper. These were notions of shape employing simple internal frames that could be visually checked. In upper Bed II times, there were no "three-dimensional" bilateral symmetries that would have required coordination of any of these concepts. By extension, it is unlikely that the hominids used any more general frames of reference.

In sum, it seems that the development of a general frame of spatial reference did not include an "affine" stage of competence in parallels, but did include the relatively early appearance of notions of interval, shape, and mirroring. Here at least, the archaeological sequence is not quite what one would expect from a strict adherence to the Piagetian sequence. Parallels appear not to have been as crucial as Piaget proposed. But in other respects the phylogenetic sequence does resemble the ontogenetic sequence, indeed in a manner I find rather striking. I refer to the development of external, as opposed to internal, frames of reference.

At one point in the child's development of concepts of space (IIa to be precise), he is unable to predict the orientation of the water level in a tilted jar. Interestingly, children often draw the water level parallel to the base of the jar, regardless of its orientation to true horizontal. When drawing poles on mountain slopes or chimneys on houses, the same children draw the figures perpendicular to the slopes, not to the horizontal or external frame (Piaget and Inhelder 1967: 382–84). They consider internal spatial orientations but not external ones. In a similar manner, I believe, the artisans in upper Bed II at Olduvai attended to internal configurations of their artifacts but had no external spatial framework to which they oriented them. I do not wish to overstate the comparison; the similarity is perhaps not even surprising. But it does suggest that a crucial step in the development of notions of space, both in ontogeny and phylogeny, was the departure from local frames of reference and the construction of a general theory of space. It is precisely the addition of a general and external reference frame that transforms the simple notions of spatial quantity, shape, and reversal into an intuitive concept of euclidean space.

Chronological Summary

In this section I will summarize as succinctly as possible the results of the preceding analysis. I will attempt to combine the perspectives of topological, projective, and euclidean geometry into a description of the intuitive spatial repertoires used by three successive groups of hominids in the manufacture of stone tools.

Spatial Concepts 2 Million Years Ago

By modern standards, the spatial repertoire of two-million-year-old stone knappers was extremely limited. It consisted almost entirely of simple topological notions like proximity, separation, and order. The hallmark of the Oldowan, the chopper, required only a concept of individual blows or trimming scars (separation), a notion of positioning one next to another (pairs), and, perhaps, a concept of the edge (boundary) dividing faces of the tool. Scrapers, on cores or flakes, required the additional notion of sequences of blows arranged according to a constant direction (order). Almost all of the Oldowan tools could have been manufactured using only these concepts. They constitute the minimum necessary spatial competence.

But the Oldowan is not a "topology only" technology. Some of the artifacts, particularly the tools termed awls, demonstrate attention to the shape of the edge *in plan*. This suggests that the hominids did, in fact, distinguish between curvilinear and rectilinear shapes, and this distinction is *not* a topological one. Indeed, it is one of the prerequisites of euclidean notions.

There appears to have been little attention to the overall shape of Oldowan tools. It was the configuration of edges that was the goal of these stone knappers. Topological notions with the addition of a distinction between rectilinear (especially "pointy") and curvilinear (smooth) shapes can produce a wide range of working edges. Indeed, if mechanical effectiveness is the intent, these spatial notions can produce edges to perform virtually all tasks asked of a stone technology. The hominids appear to have made no attempt to alter the overall shape of the tools, for whatever reason. Such attention to overall shape is a characteristic of succeeding technologies.

Spatial Concepts 1.2 Million Years Ago

The spatial repertoire of hominids living 1.2 million years ago contained all of the concepts used during the Oldowan, plus some new ones.

The first of these is the notion of interval, or a constant quantity of space. 1.2-million-year-old assemblages include very circular discoids and very round spheroids. These require, at a minimum, a notion of diameter or radius, which are both constant amounts of space used as an internal reference. This "quantity of space" need not have been some constant and arbitrary measurement, but could simply have been one edge-to-edge distance used as a reference for the others. In all cases in this time period the knapper could have used direct observation to choose an amount and compare it to other intervals. Such a notion of spatial quantity is not entailed by topological concepts.

A second spatial notion that appears at this time is that of symmetry. It was not a full-scale euclidean symmetry of mirrored congruency, but it did include the mirroring of shapes. These mirrored shapes were, in a sense, "similar" shapes. They retained the same basic configuration of curves, recurves, shoulders, and so on, in the absence of true congruency. Such shapes result from distinctions similar to the curvilinear/rectilinear distinction exhibited by Oldowan artifacts. But the important notion here is that of reversal, which is in fact a topological notion, but one that is more sophisticated than those needed for the Oldowan.

Both the notion of interval and the notion of symmetry contributed to the development of the idea of the artifact as a whole. No longer did hominids focus attention only on the edge; they attempted to attain certain overall shapes. Discoids, spheroids, and bifaces all required some notion of overall design. But the set of conceptual tools for achieving this aim was still relatively primitive. Reversal and interval are purely internal frames of reference. They were capable of creating two-dimensional shapes that could be directly perceived and whose constituent elements could be visually compared to the reference. The one three-dimensional whole, the sphere, is relatively simple and can be produced by visual comparison. Significantly, nothing resembling regular cross sections or other complex three-dimensional shapes can be found in this time period. The spatial wholes consist only of internal frames of reference. There appears to have been no general organization of space that extended beyond the artifact at hand.

Spatial Concepts 300,000 Years Ago

By 300,000 years ago there is evidence for an essentially modern concept of space, one that extended beyond the individual framework of the artifact and organized space as a whole. Again, all of the spatial concepts required for earlier tools are evident 300,000 years ago. Added to these are several important notions.

Perhaps the most critical new spatial concept is the understanding and coordination of multiple points of view. The intentionally straight edges and parallels on some of the Isimila bifaces require attention to a stable point of view, which is a projective notion. More complex still are the regular cross sections of many of these bifaces. Regular cross sections in three dimensions require attention to multiple perspectives or viewpoints, most of which are not perceptually available and must be imagined. Unlike the spatial concepts used for earlier tools, these projective notions allow the internal frame of the artifact to be controlled by the external relation of perspective.

A second spatial concept to appear by 300,000 years ago is that of a "euclidean" space, that is, a space definable by a three-dimensional coordinate grid. It is not necessary, of course, that space be thought of in such formal terms. What is necessary is that space be organized using a notion of spatial quantity (congruency, for example) and that all of space be organized in this fashion. The congruent symmetries of Isimila bifaces provide ample evidence of a fairly strict adherence

to spatial quantity. Arguments for an infinitely extendable euclidean space require a leap of inference, because we have only the artifacts and not their arrangements. Nevertheless, the excellent three-
dimensional symmetries of some of the handaxes suggest that the
spatial organization of these hominids was the intuitive equivalent of
a euclidean space, and that this framework was a general one extend-
ing beyond the internal framework of single artifacts to organize
space as a whole.

The third spatial concept to appear by 300,000 years ago is a topological one, and evidence for it comes not from fine congruent symmetries but from minimally trimmed artifacts. This is the notion of
whole-part relations, the understanding of the spatial relationship of
a whole to its constituent parts. The minimally trimmed bifaces required an idea of final shape (which could include the euclidean
notions discussed above) and also an awareness of the minimum
modifications required to achieve that shape. The knapper had to
understand how each *possible* modification would affect the result, and
choose accordingly. Trial-and-error knapping, even with constant
checking, would be insufficient.

All of these spatial notions combine into a sophisticated repertoire
for stone knapping. The means of achieving desired shapes were
much more effective than those evident at 1.2 million. The hominids
employed artifact designs that required perspective, the control of
spatial quantity, and an understanding of composition, in the sense of
constituent elements. Like earlier hominids they had an idea of final
shape, but, unlike their earlier counterparts, they had a sophisticated
array of spatial concepts for conceiving and attaining the desired result. These projective and euclidean concepts would appear to be sufficient to account for all of the stone tools archaeologists know of or,
indeed, can imagine. Stone tools of later times are different and,
arguably, more specialized in function. But their spatial prerequisites are no more complex than those we can recognize by 300,000
years ago.

Two Landmarks in Spatial Competence

In the preceding summary, my intention was to describe the spatial
concepts necessary for the manufacture of stone tools at three points
in human evolution. I would now like to take a slightly more dynamic
approach and try to distill from this description some of the actual
conceptual acquisitions that resulted in the evolution of spatial abilities between two million and 300,000 years ago. It is my contention
that spatial concepts did not accrue in additive fashion, like the

reading of a geometry text, but were acquired in constellations of concepts tied, ultimately, to single overriding ideas or conceptual breakthroughs. These breakthroughs were unlikely to have resulted from conscious theorizing on the part of individual hominids. They were, rather, developments within the repertoire of day-to-day spatial strategies that yielded more pleasing or desirable results. Nevertheless, these developments opened up many new possibilities for artifact form.

The artifactual evidence argues, I believe, for two such landmark acquisitions—the notions of overall shape and external perspective.

Prior to either of these developments, hominid tools were very simple. Oldowan hominids attended to the nature of the edge—probably tied to a specific task at hand—and paid no attention to the overall shape of their tools. These edges required, as we have seen, only rudimentary spatial concepts. Indeed, in many respects these tools resemble tools made by modern chimpanzees. Both have simple modifications tied to an immediate task, and both are spatially simple. The major differences are the medium (though some chimps do use stone hammers) and the task. But in terms of spatial concepts, Oldowan tools look very ape-like.

The acquisition that first takes hominid tools out of range of ape spatial concepts is the notion of overall shape, or, to put it a bit differently, some conception of the tool as a whole. While the edge-oriented technology of the Oldowan appears to have been tied to immediate tasks at hand (an *ad hoc* technology), the presence of tools with repeated, overall shape suggests that in these cases, an idea of the whole tool existed previously in the mind of the knapper. The biface is a tool with a definite two-dimensional shape and, moreover, a shape that was repeated again and again. True, the appearance of the biface coincides with the appearance of a technique for manufacturing large flakes (Jones 1981). This technique does not, however, also entail the further modifications so often seen. We do not know why these 1.2-million-year-old hominids strived to attain this particular shape, but we do know some of the shape's conceptual requirements.

The first of these requirements is some notion of intended result, even if at first the means for achieving that intention were rather primitive. Again, this is a marked change from a purely *ad hoc* technology in which a knapper chipped on an appropriately sized stone until he recognized a usable edge. With bifaces, the whole tool, more or less, had to be conceived ahead of time. But the kind of spatial concepts necessary for an *ad hoc*, edge-directed technology— proximity, order, and so on—are insufficient to direct trimming for the achievement of an overall shape. Some kind of internal reference frame is necessary. This, then, is the second concept required for biface manufacture. There appear, initially, to have been two spatial notions involved here: interval and symmetry. However primitive from our perspective, these notions were capable of directing the positioning of trimming blows so that a roughly regular, two-dimensional shape could be attained.

While the idea of artifact- or object-as-a-whole may seem painfully rudimentary, it represents a much more comprehensive organization of space than that used in the Oldowan. Simple spatial notions like order and separation had now become elements arranged into higher-level patterns. Moreover, these patterns could be repeated again and again because they existed as specific intentions. Technology could exist apart from a specific task at hand, and, indeed, had come to occupy a conceptual realm of its own.

The second constellation of spatial concepts includes euclidean and projective notions, along with a more sophisticated understanding of the relation of whole to parts. The acquisition of this constellation appears to have hinged on a single breakthrough in spatial thinking—the invention or discovery of perspective. This projective notion was the key that allowed the extension of internal spatial frames that were anchored to specific objects into general constructions of space that organized possible as well as real positions. Such general constructions, like euclidean space, require a notion of interval or amount of space and some means of orienting these intervals. As we can see from the early bifaces from West Natron and Olduvai, a notion of interval was in use fairly early, but there is no evidence of general frames of reference. Intervals are, by themselves, insufficient. What is required as well is a constant orientation, and such constant orientation is impossible without some notion of viewpoints that exist independent of that of ego. One must be able to step away from the tyranny imposed by direct perception and construct alternative views. This is quite a conceptual feat, requiring complex substitutions and restructuring of shapes. Moreover, it requires the subjugation of what one actually sees to what one thinks.

I do not think it a coincidence that evidence for three-dimensional symmetries, congruency, and other euclidean notions appears in the archaeological record at the same time as evidence for projective straight lines and regular cross sections. It was precisely the acquisition of projective understanding that transformed the internal frames of earlier periods into general organizations of space. Indeed, of the two spatial notions necessary for a euclidean space, one, the notion of interval, is relatively primitive and early, while the other, the notion of perspective, is relatively sophisticated and late.

While the two developments I have just discussed—the concept of artifact-as-a-whole and the understanding of perspective—may appear rather different from one another, they do share two important similarities. First, they both require that simpler spatial notions be coordinated into higher-level conceptions. The notion of artifact-as-a-whole requires coordination of such notions as separation, reversal, and the distinction between curvilinear and rectilinear. Perspective requires coordinating images of the artifact along with masking, order, and reversal. Second, each of these developments marks a further divorcing of space from the focus of ego. Oldowan artifacts need not have had conceptual existence beyond the immediate action of ego tied to the task at hand. There need not have been an idea of "chopper" or "scraper" or "awl" as a thing separate from the action of the hominid at his task. But the existence of overall shapes requires that the object as a whole be conceived as somehow separate from the action of ego, that is, as a thing with its own existence. Again, this seems terribly rudimentary, but it is a crucial step, I think, in the development of human-like technology. The development of perspective is an even more dramatic refocusing. The construction of perspective requires a complete "stepping out" of the bonds of perception. One must construct not just objects in space but also the *viewpoints* those separate objects might have when looking back at ego. Objects *and* ego can then be conceived as occupying the same space.

The evolution of these concepts of space reflects, I think, the development of a very distinct concept of self as an actor in an independently existing world. Such an awareness is at the heart of human understanding.

Archaeological Implications

The results of this analysis of spatial competence bear directly on several traditional archaeological concerns. Perhaps most important, they add to our understanding of technological evolution in general. They are also relevant to specific questions of culture history in the early Stone Age.

The best-known conclusion of Stone Age archaeology is that tools and tool assemblages became more complex over the course of two million years. This trend combines many aspects of technological behavior. Specialization of task (Dennell 1983) and efficiency of raw material (the "inches of cutting edge per kilo" argument, for example) are two favorites of general reviews (Holloway 1981, for example). Another aspect of complexity is a rather vague idea often called "refinement." The tools simply look prettier over time. Part of this is a result of changes in technique, such as the use of soft hammers in stone knapping (Bordes 1968). But much of it is a consequence of more sophisticated and modern concepts of space. Oldowan tools are crude because there is no overall concept of shape and no use of perspective and general spatial frames—two spatial notions almost always used in making modern tools. Later Acheulean handaxes often look "fine" to us precisely because the knappers used spatial ideas and standards that were essentially modern. This crude-to-fine evolution has little to do with function or specialization or efficiency. It was a consequence of the evolution of spatial competence.

The evolution of spatial competence also provides some additional clues to three questions of early culture history: the transition from Oldowan to early Acheulean, the problem of the Developed Oldowan, and the question of evolutionary stasis in the Middle Pleistocene.

Biface industries appear relatively suddenly in East Africa (Leakey 1971; Clark and Kurashina 1979). In most areas no gradual transition between the earlier Oldowan and the biface-using Acheulean can be traced (but see Chavaillon et al. 1979). The abruptness of the change may be due partially to gaps in the stratigraphic sequence, especially the disconformity in Bed II at Olduvai. Nevertheless, the biface assemblages are distinctive, and no gradual technological change out of the Oldowan has been documented. The invention of a technique for manufacturing large flakes accounts for part of the difference (Jones 1981), but there are also early bifaces on cores. As we have seen, there is a significant difference between the spatial concepts used on earlier Oldowan tools and those used on the later bifaces, a difference that is enough to take biface technology outside the range of ape behavior. The spatial evidence amplifies the distinction between Oldowan and Acheulean, and, if no transitional industries are found, supports arguments that biface culture originated elsewhere and was introduced into East Africa from its area of origin.

From the point of view of spatial competence, Developed Oldowan bifaces are indistinguishable from early Acheulean bifaces. Mary Leakey (various, e.g. 1971) has argued that the Developed Oldowan assemblages from Olduvai and elsewhere, which have some bifaces but mostly flakes, choppers, and other "Oldowan" elements, were a separate culture from the Acheulean, perhaps were even made by a separate species. If both the Developed Oldowan and the early Acheulean required the same spatial concepts, and if both are outside the range of ape behavior to the same degree, then Leakey's argument for separate species, at least, is seriously weakened.

Recently, arguments have been made for the evolutionary stasis of *Homo erectus* (Rightmire 1981), arguments that have a parallel in technology. If one looks at the range of tool types, very little changes between the first appearance of biface assemblages (1.5 million years ago) and the end of the Acheulean (about 200,000 years ago). Moreover, we find much the same range of tools in many parts of the Old World. This suggests a cultural stasis of sorts. However, when we consider spatial competence, we find that a very significant development occurred after 1.5 million and before 300,000 years ago. This was the development of sophisticated notions of perspective and of general frames of reference. Indeed, this was the single most dramatic development in the evolution of human spatial thinking, and it appeared sometime in the middle of the supposed period of stasis. This is not necessarily an argument that deflates the entire punctuationalist view of human evolution. But it does weaken the argument for behavioral stasis in the Middle Pleistocene.

PART II:

The Evolution of Intelligence

Introduction

The preceding analysis and conclusions are, I believe, interesting in their own right. They have revealed something about the development of various intuitive geometries and, from another perspective, have explained why some tool assemblages appear crude and others fine. But as a prehistorian I would like to show more about the minds of early hominids than just the specific spatial concepts they employed to make tools. Prehistory is an ambitious discipline; we reconstruct entire subsistence systems from fragmentary bones, and religious systems from painted caves. Can we not also extrapolate from a knowledge of spatial concepts to a knowledge of overall intellectual ability? That is, can we not use these spatial concepts to document the evolution of intelligence in general? I am, of course, assuming that there is such a thing as "general" intelligence. This is in fact a debatable point whose alternatives have interesting implications for the preceding analysis (Atran 1982). I cannot pretend to resolve this issue, and will pursue only the implications that my analysis has within the context of a general theory of intelligence.

There are two ways to use spatial concepts to argue for general intelligence—through common sense and through formal theory. It is tempting to speculate on general behavior from narrow conclusions about spatial ability. For instance, one could argue, based on the presence of spatial perspective, that the hominids were also capable of complex interpersonal relationships that depended on recognition of another's social viewpoint. This seems a reasonable extension of the ability to "step out" of one's immediate perception. But, while "reasonable," such an argument is based at best on vague, commonsense understandings of spatial ability, social ability, and their common basis in the even vaguer concept of intelligence. What appears reasonable on the surface becomes problematic when scrutinized. Unfortunately, much interpretive prehistory is no more soundly based than this—reasonable interpretations based on commonsense understandings. These are simply insufficient. The alternative is to base one's interpretation on established theories of behavior, in this case theories of intelligence.

A review of prevailing theories of intelligence is far beyond the scope of this volume. Indeed, the concept of intelligence is itself a commonsense notion that encompasses a wide range of behaviors. Pinning down a universally acceptable definition is impossible. As a consequence, theories of intelligence tend to narrow the range of appropriate behavior and to attend to rather different kinds of evidence. For example, psychometric approaches emphasize relative performance on standardized tests, while Piagetian approaches emphasize verbal accounts and errors in performance. "Each major approach has evolved procedures for selecting which aspects of intellect to focus upon, which types of issues to raise, which methodological procedures to apply to analyzing findings, and which representational languages to use to characterize them. There may be no overall maximally effective approach but rather several local maximums: approaches that are optimal given constraints on other features" (Siegler and Richards 1982:900).

For a theory of intelligence to be appropriate to prehistory, it must do two things. First, it must define intelligence in a way that encompasses the behavior of non-humans. It must see intelligence as an entity that varies from taxon to taxon and that can evolve within a single taxon over time. The theory must be capable of describing the differences between taxa, especially apes and humans, and of measuring these differences in some way. Second, the theory must be able to assess the end products of behavior. With very few exceptions, the archaeological record lacks sequences of behavior. Most of the evidence of prehistory consists of consequences of behavior, some intended, some not. The theory must be able to deal with consequences and products, though it need not have been designed specifically to do so. Many approaches to intelligence cannot meet these two requirements. Psychometric approaches (IQ, for example) measure differences in performance on standardized tests, and, while perhaps useful in predicting success in school, make no sense (or claims!) in the context of evolution. We cannot give apes or Neanderthals the Stanford-Binet. And while psychometric approaches do assess results, these results are very specialized and are certainly not found in prehistory. Information-processing theories, on the other hand, often rely on modeling sequences of behavior used in problem solving. Here the difficulty lies in sequences, for we cannot observe them in prehistory.* A third constraint is also important in choosing an appropriate theory: the theory must be persuasive. The categories of intelligence it defines need to have been confirmed again and again, preferably in cross-cultural and comparative studies as well as in Western classrooms. The truth and reliability of the theory must be established using contemporary data; only then can the theory be applied to prehistory. The archaeological record does not have the resolution to generate and test theories of intelligence on its own.

Piagetian Theory

Piagetian theory fulfills the conditions listed above. It is evolutionary in scope, it can assess the products of behavior, and it is persuasive. Indeed, it is arguably the most broadly applied theory of intelligence yet developed. It is also continually under scrutiny, by both sympathetic and unsympathetic scholars, and many of its results remain controversial. I will not attempt a detailed exegesis of sixty years of Piagetian research. Instead, I will present a very broad overview of the theory's major features, emphasizing those that make the Piagetian approach especially useful to studies of evolution.

Piagetian theory is a structural theory, a structure here being a principle or set of principles actively employed by an organism to organize its behavior. In Piagetian theory these structures are, ultimately, physiological patterns in the brain; that is, they have a biological reality and are not simply convenient models or heuristic devices (Piaget 1974). There are, of course, many structural theories of behavior, from Dumezil's treatment of Indo-European myth (Littleton 1967) to Chomskian generative syntax. Some, like Chomskian theories, concentrate on structural patterns coded in the genome. But such genetic structures are not what Piaget had in mind. Indeed, his approach is more properly termed a constructivist one, and it is the constructivist aspects of his theory that are perhaps most important.

An individual does not inherit his or her organizational principles or structures. Rather, they are *constructed* during ontogeny. Certain rudimentary and simple patterns are inherited—sucking and gripping, for example. But soon the infant elaborates these patterns into more complex ones, which have never been "hard wired" in the genome. In using the primitive structures, the infant encounters situations in which they are insufficient. This conflict requires a reorganization of the original principles into more comprehensive structures.

---

*Information-processing theories may have some potential in assessing *reconstructed* sequences in stone knapping. The theories would depend on the reliability of the reconstructions.

For example, gripping and arm waving are coordinated into a pattern of pulling objects close for examination. This process of insufficiency ("disequilibrium," in Piagetian terms), conflict, and reorganization ("equilibration") continues throughout ontogeny and results in more and more complex principles of organization. It is important to emphasize that these new principles are not learned in a simple behaviorist sense. An individual must actively apply his or her structures, and reorganize them when they fail; he or she does not simply ingest new solutions from the outside. Action is essential. This constructivist approach is at the heart of Piagetian theory and, in truth, presents some knotty problems when applied to phylogeny (see below). However, it is the stage aspects of the theory that are best known, and probably also the most abused.

Piagetian theory is a stage theory. Each stage consists of a more or less consistent set of organizing principles that the child applies across all behavioral domains. The stages are qualitatively distinct from one another and are not heuristic conveniences, but, according to the theory, constitute stable, if temporary, types of reasoning. Children pass from one stage to the next when they find that their current type of reasoning fails in more and more circumstances, and, over time, they complete a wholesale reorganization of the underlying principles. The sequence of stages is invariant—no stage can be skipped—because the principles typical of one stage provide the base out of which children construct the principles of the next stage. All children pass through the stages and substages in the same order, though the precise age at which children achieve a particular stage varies considerably.

Piaget defined the stages in terms of qualitative criteria. Piagetian method is based on observation and on dialogue between experimenter and child, with special emphasis placed on the reasons children give for their solutions. Children give "rational" explanations for their errors (assuming, of course, that one uses their style of reasoning). This kind of method is very different from the quantitative techniques of the psychometric approach, and is responsible for much of the naive criticism of Piaget. However, the method is replicable, and, more importantly, its results have been replicated by many different experimenters in many different contexts.

The dialogue aspects of Piagetian method cannot of course be used in prehistory, and this seriously reduces the resolution of any analysis. It is especially difficult to distinguish substages without the subjects' verbal reasons for certain solutions. However, a number of Piagetian "tasks" yield patterns of objects that are typical of certain stages. In particular, Piaget placed considerable emphasis on the development of spatial thinking (Piaget and Inhelder 1967; Inhelder, Piaget, and Szeminska 1960). Piaget and Barbel Inhelder made extensive studies of the way children organized objects, copied figures, described scenes, found their way home from school, and so on. Much of my earlier discussion of topological, projective, and euclidean concepts is heavily influenced by their discussion of these behaviors. In this sense my earlier analysis is not unbiased. Nevertheless, the Piagetian reliance on spatial thinking makes the theory capable of assessing early tools.

Piagetian theory posits four major stages of intellectual development: sensorimotor, preoperational, concrete operations, and formal operations.

Sensorimotor intelligence is organized action. It consists of both simple and complex patterns of action and movement in the absence of any internalized, representational thought. It is the intelligence of infants. The most rudimentary organizational principle, and also the earliest, is the biological rhythm. Gripping, sucking, and arm waving are examples of rhythmically controlled actions performed spontaneously by infants. These "reflexes" and rhythms are inherited. But very soon after birth, the child coordinates these primitive organizing principles into more complex patterns, termed "schemes." "A scheme is the structure or organization of actions as they are transferred or generalized by repetition in similar or analogous circumstances" (Piaget and Inhelder 1969:4). For example, the infant coordinates gripping, arm swinging, and sucking, and transfers them into a scheme of sucking objects as a means of investigation. The infant can then coordinate this scheme into more complex ones like simple games, and so on. By the end of the sensorimotor stage, the infant has constructed an impressive repertoire of action schemes.

Sensorimotor intelligence is an intelligence of immediate, physical action. Because the infant cannot represent action in thought, the patterns are restricted to "real time" sequences. Physical action can only be successive; one action happens after another. As a consequence, sensorimotor schemes are also successive. At best, one action can only be chained to another, and in no sense can an infant conceive of the entire sequence simultaneously. A scheme can be "in thought" only "in action"; hence the repetitious character of much of infant behavior. Theirs is a world organized entirely by their action.

Action schemes are not only found in the behavior of infants. They are, in fact, an almost ubiquitous kind of intelligence found throughout animal behavior, including that of human adults. Many adult sports, for example, are based upon schemes of action. In baseball, the batter has no time to *reflect* upon the velocity and trajectory of a

95-mile-per-hour fastball. He must put into operation a complex sequence of physical action, learned not by conscious reasoning, but by constant, numbing repetition. When Pete Rose bats, he uses the same kind of intelligence that a cheetah uses to bring down a gazelle, or, though less polished, an infant uses to play "patty cake." As such, sensorimotor intelligence forms the base of the Piagetian sequence. It is only when an infant (or other organism) represents action *in thought* that a new and more powerful intelligence is in force.

The preoperational stage is the least clearly defined of the four major stages. As the name implies, thinking typical of this stage lacks the important features of operational thought. Indeed, in some ways the organization is more like that of sensorimotor intelligence. But there is one crucial hallmark of this stage—the ability to perform action *in thought*. This representational ability is the same one that allows the development of semiotic behavior such as language.* The preoperational child can, by using this representational ability, describe a sequence of actions he or she has just performed. To do this, the child must be able to repeat them in thought—repetition divorced from the action itself. The child can also project a sequence of action into the future. Here we encounter one of the limitations of preoperational thought. Preoperational thinking organizes internal imitations of action sequences and, as such, is limited to patterns that could actually be performed in real time. Because action can only be taken upon one quality of an event or object at a time, internalized action can consider only one variable at a time. One of Piaget's most famous examples is that of the clay balls. When the experimenter rolls balls of clay into sausages, the preoperational child assumes that the amount of clay has increased because the length has increased. The child has been unable to consider the qualities of length and thickness simultaneously. Interestingly, when the sausages become very thin, he or she may completely shift orientation and claim that there is now less clay. This narrow focus of preoperational reasoning has important effects on how a preoperational child plans a project. Even though the child can foresee the intended result by means of the ability to represent things not present, only one variable can be attended to at a time. The child cannot imagine contingencies, only straightforward sequences. As a consequence, he or she can only monitor by trial and error, that is, proceed until failure, then begin a new imagined sequence, and so on.

The preoperational stage is perhaps best understood as the transi-

*Piaget's treatment of language itself is one of his most controversial, and, perhaps fortunately, need not concern us in detail.

tion between the pure action of sensorimotor intelligence and the logical power of operational intelligence. Continuous development occurs throughout this stage; indeed, the same developments occur, in the same order, as during the sensorimotor stage, but this time they occur within thought. It is often convenient to subdivide the preoperational stage into two substages, the symbolic and the intuitive. In the symbolic substage, the child possesses representational ability, but his thinking remains closely tied to his own possible action. Thought in the intuitive substage is less centered on ego, and the child understands that objects or events can act independent of his participation (Piaget 1960; 1972). Again, these substages are merely convenient divisions of a continuous development. Piaget himself occasionally subdivided the stage differently (e.g., Piaget 1973). The same general organizational features exist throughout the stage.

Operational thought is the intelligence of modern adults. In Piaget's scheme there are actually two stages of operational intelligence—concrete and formal—but both share a number of characteristics that distinguish them from preoperational intelligence. An operation is a principle, used to organize thought (ultimately internalized action), that has powerful organizational features, features that allow an individual to transcend the limitations of "real time," one-variable thinking. The two fundamental features of operations are reversibility and conservation. "Operations . . . are actions coordinated into reversible systems in such a way that each operation corresponds to a possible operation that renders it void" (Piaget 1971:36). There are two kinds of reversibility—inversion and reciprocity. Inversion entails inverting a transformation and by so doing returning to the starting point. For example, in arithmetic one may subtract a number as well as add it ($+A-A=0$). Reciprocity is simply a reversal of order, such as $A \geq B$, $B \geq A$, therefore $A = B$. Such a transformation yields an equivalence rather than a negation, but both are means of returning to a starting point in thought. Reversibility is a very useful organizational tool, and an extended example is in order. I will use one of Piaget's favorites—the quaternary group.

An experimenter shows a subject a moving object that is intermittently starting and stopping. When the object stops, a bulb lights up. How are these two phenomena related? If the subject uses reversible operations, he will reason roughly as follows. The lighting of the bulb could cause the object to stop. I will call this relation A. This "hypothesis" would be disproved if the bulb ever lit up without the object's stopping, a relation I will call B. Here the subject is using inversion, that is, a negation. Alternatively, the stopping of the object could cause the bulb to light up (relation C). This is a reciprocal, or reversal of order, of relation A, which can in turn be negated (inverted) if the object stops without the bulb's lighting up (relation D). Relation D does not, of course, disprove relation A. If the subject coordinates all of these reversibilities, he can solve the problem without error very quickly. Preoperational thinking could only attend to one-way sequences, and only by accident arrive at the true causal relationship. This ability to return to a starting point in thought is crucial to operational thinking, and, indeed, is behind such well-known operational understandings as conservation.

Conservation is arguably Piaget's most famous concept. In transitivity, when $A = B$ and $B = C$, A must equal C. Something has been conserved across the relationship. Preoperational children do not see any logical necessity in transitivity, and, at least at first, insist that they must directly compare A and C before they can know. Conservation results from an ability to coordinate many variables simultaneously (as in the bulb example). In the example of the clay balls cited earlier, a child using operational organizations is able to "conserve" the quantity by compensating for the change in one variable with that of another.

Reversibility and conservation provide operational thinking with some very useful organizational features. One is pre-correction of errors. "What this means is that an operational system is one which excludes errors before they are made, because every operation has its inverse in the system . . ." (Piaget 1970:15). With operational thinking an individual can make detailed contingency plans by, in a sense, returning to a starting point in thought after anticipating possible difficulties. Unlike the preoperational thinker, he need not proceed by trial and error but can anticipate errors ahead of time and plan accordingly. It is the back-and-forth, two-way organization allowed by reversibility that provides this advantage over the one-way, action-mimicking organization of preoperational thought.

There are two operational stages in Piaget's scheme. While both use reversibility, conservation, pre-correction of errors, and so on, there is, according to Piaget, a marked difference in the power and scope of these organizing principles. Concrete operations, the first to appear, are used to organize tangible things like objects, people, and simple concepts like numbers and time—hence the term "concrete." Hypothetical entities and abstract concepts are not the stuff of concrete operations. Using concrete operations, one can classify objects according to color, and reclassify them according to shape (true classification requires reversibility: $A + A' = B$, $B - A' = A$). However, concrete operations do not encompass such concepts as "class of all classes." Using concrete operations, one accepts division as the inverse of multiplication, but sees no necessity (or sense!) in $\sqrt{-1}$. Concrete operations are, nevertheless, a very powerful organizing tool and, indeed, are the principal organizational tool for day-to-day living. Tasks, tools, kinship, politics, and religion are all organized in this manner.

The structures of formal operational thinking are more generally applied than those of concrete operations. While one uses concrete operations to organize real objects and events, one uses formal operations to generalize about all possible situations of objects and events. This includes the capacity for hypothetico-deductive reasoning, the use of propositional logic, and the ability to dissociate form from content. In other words, formal operations are characteristic of the most sophisticated kind of reasoning we know. It is the final stage of Piaget's scheme and also the most controversial.

In addition to his general claims for hypothetical reasoning, Piaget argues for a more specific change in the logic of formal operations. While concrete operations employ the two kinds of reversibility, inversion and reciprocity, formal operations coordinate them. The solution to the "bulb and object" example used above was a formal operational solution, because inversion and reciprocity were coordinated. Another well-known Piagetian task involves the use of a balance. An individual using formal operations knows that a balance can be achieved by adding or subtracting weight (inversion), by moving the weights in or out on the arms (reciprocity), or by adding weight to one arm and moving a smaller weight further out on the other (a coordination of the two). After only brief experimentation, the formal operational thinker can generalize the properties to all possible situations. An individual using concrete operations can balance the scale by adding or moving weight, but does not construct a system of proportions that he sees as being always and everywhere true. It is not that the concrete operational thinker cannot balance the weights, only that he has no foolproof system.

Having briefly reviewed the Piagetian approach to intelligence, we can now see why it is a useful theory for studies of the evolution of intelligence.

First of all, it is evolutionary in scope. While Piaget's scheme of stages has been applied largely to human ontogeny, it has also proved a useful tool for studying comparative intelligence. The substages of sensorimotor and also preoperational intelligence have been identified in non-human primates (e.g., Parker 1976; Redshaw 1978; Parker and Gibson 1979). As with all taxonomies, there is a temptation to focus on shared characteristics and to ignore differences. Apes are not human children, and, even though these researchers take great pains to make this point, there is a danger of caricaturing their results. The studies do demonstrate that there is some descriptive truth to Piaget's scheme and, moreover, that it can be used as a comparative language. Piaget's emphasis on organization and complexity of organized behavior allows his work to be extended beyond human behavior. Indeed, it was always his intention that his theory be a general theory of development, applicable to all sequences of logical development, including ontogeny, the history of science, and phylogeny.

> The fundamental hypothesis of genetic epistemology is that there is a parallelism between the progress made in the logical and rational organization of knowledge and the corresponding formative psychological processes. Well, now, if that is our hypothesis, what will be our field of study? Of course, the most fruitful, most obvious field of study would be reconstituting human prehistory—the history of human thinking in prehistoric man. Unfortunately, we are not very well informed about the psychology of Neanderthal man or about the psychology of *Homo siniensis* of Teilhard de Chardin. Since this field of biogenesis is not available to us, we shall do what biologists do and turn to ontogenesis. Nothing could be more accessible to study than the ontogenesis of these notions. There are children all around us. It is with children that we have the best chance of studying the development of logical knowledge, mathematical knowledge, physical knowledge and so forth [Piaget 1970:13].

Piaget's theory can be applied to prehistory. It can be used to assess some of the behaviors visible in the archaeological record primarily because it is capable of assessing results of certain kinds of action. Not all of Piaget's criteria or methods are applicable, of course. Much of Piaget's technique relies on dialogue between experimenter and subject, and many of the subdivisions within stages are based on the manner in which a child achieves a particular result. Such techniques and distinctions cannot be applied to prehistory. However, Piaget, especially in his work with Barbel Inhelder, placed a great deal of emphasis on spatial concepts, and many of these can be assessed on the basis of the products of action. Archaeologists have stone tools in abundance, and the manufacture of stone tools required spatial concepts. It is here that we have the most direct application of Piagetian method to prehistory. A second advantage of Piagetian method is its reliance on qualitative assessments. We can base our analysis of spatial concepts on relatively few artifacts, and do not need the large samples required of quantitatively based methods. The latter would be almost useless in prehistory, where samples are often small, and selected by the vagaries of preservation rather than by a rigorous statistical technique.

The third requirement of a prehistorically useful theory of intelligence is that it be persuasive. I would be extremely remiss if I were to imply that Piagetian theory is universally true or without critics, or that the criticisms were irrelevant to this study. The theory has been criticized on methodological grounds (especially for sample size and use of qualitative measures), on epistemological grounds (especially for the notion of stages), and on grounds of obscurity. However, many parts of the theory have held up remarkably well under massive testing, and, while its ambitious goal of a universal model of reasoning and development is unmet, it remains perhaps the most reliable general theory of intelligence yet proposed. Nevertheless, two criticisms of Piagetian theory as an *evolutionary* theory need to be addressed more specifically—that it is recapitulationist and Lamarckian.

As I mentioned above, Piagetian theory has been used in comparative studies and, based on this evidence, has also been used to reconstruct the phylogeny of intelligence (Parker and Gibson 1979 is probably the best example). Here we run headlong into a scientific controversy of long standing: the nature of the parallel between ontogeny and phylogeny. Piaget maintained that his ontogenetic sequence was directly parallel to the phylogenetic sequence. Gould (1977) traces this idea to the Haeckelian biology of Piaget's youth (Piaget's first publications were in biology, the earliest dating to 1907, when he was eleven years old). Such recapitulationist thinking is at odds with most current evolutionary programs, which discount any direct relationship between ontogeny and phylogeny (though they acknowledge some general parallels). Indeed, for many current scholars, any mention of ontogeny and phylogeny in the same text invites immediate derision. Gould (1977) has argued, convincingly I believe, that such naive rejection is unwarranted and that the parallel between ontogeny and phylogeny can be a useful source of understanding. Of course, he too rejects a narrow recapitulationist position—terminal addition with acceleration—and specifically criticizes Piaget's approach. From the Piagetian perspective, the source of the parallel lies in the constructivist nature of intelligence. The structure typical of one stage is a logically necessary prerequisite for the next. The succeeding stage builds on and out of the organization of its antecedent. This logical necessity must be true of any sequence, including both ontogeny and phylogeny. The parallel is logically entailed, and need not be the result of some biological connection between the two processes of development.

Piaget was not a Darwinian, nor was he really a Lamarckian, though naive criticism occasionally makes the latter claim. Piaget aimed at integrating both approaches in his general theory of development (Piaget 1974). His goal was to generalize the mechanisms he had identified in ontogeny—assimilation, accommodation, equilibration—into a mechanism for phylogeny as well. He argued that Darwinism was pure assimilation (the organism incorporating aspects of the environment) and Lamarckism pure accommodation (the organism changing to fit the environment). His solution to the problem is interesting, but reads more like a philosophical essay than a scientific treatise. As a vision of a general theory of development, it deserves reading. However, as a practical, working model for phylogenetic development, it fails. It simply does not fit with evolutionary mechanisms as we currently understand them. I am unwilling to conclude that Piaget and evolutionary theory must remain forever unreconciled, but as both currently stand, they are incompatible.

Given the problem of Piaget's recapitulationism and the incompatibility of his evolutionary program with current theory, how is it that we can turn to Piagetian theory as a source of evolutionary understanding? The answer lies in his definition of a taxonomy of reasoning. Despite its weaknesses, Piagetian theory has described in rough outline a scheme of categories of reasoning that, in many realms of behavior, has a kernel of truth. Moreover, these categories of reasoning do appear to develop in an invariant sequence (Siegler and Richards 1982). There is no need to suppose a connection between ontogeny and phylogeny. We can apply Piaget's categories to the evolutionary evidence and let the chips fall where they may. Piagetian theory provides one of the few yardsticks of intelligence that can be applied to evolution. In other words, we can accept his descriptive conclusions without having to accept his evolutionary program.

The summary that follows is organized chronologically into four periods: Oldowan, early Acheulean, later Acheulean, and post-Acheulean. For each period, I attempt an assessment of intelligence using Piagetian theory, including the stage concepts. A more speculative summary follows the specific assessments.

The Intelligence of Oldowan Hominids

We can use Piagetian theory in two ways in an analysis of Oldowan artifacts. First, Piaget's emphasis on action as a source of concepts is a very useful way to look at stone knapping and the evolution of spatial thinking. Second, Piaget's description of preoperational reasoning encompasses all of the spatial abilities we can recognize in the Oldowan.

This suggests that Oldowan hominids were not much more intelligent than modern apes.

We construct the space we live in. Our concepts of space are neither perceived passively nor innate. Rather, we construct our concepts of space from our own actions. It is obvious that all action takes place in space of some sort; what is perhaps not obvious is that our actions in space are, ultimately, the only way we can apprehend that space. According to Piagetian theory, even our most sophisticated concepts of the structure of space result from the coordination of internalized schemes of action, schemes that were initially very primitive. From this viewpoint, the sequence of competence in topological relations makes a good deal of sense, both for the ontogenetic sequence described by Piaget and, as I hope to show, for the phyletic sequence as well.

Very young children are unable to copy geometric figures of any sort. They merely scribble. But this scribbling is itself informative, especially compared to later developments. It is rhythmic action. One action is repeated again and again, then stopped, and then another is repeated again and again. The scribbling child does not coordinate the rhythmic actions into more complex schemes. At this point, the child's conception of space is primitive and unordered. The first significant attempt at copying results in figures that reproduce only rudimentary topological relations. This occurs after the child has had experience in the act of scribbling. "The question of technique presents itself in quite simple terms. It is a matter of arresting or interrupting the primitive rhythms of scribbling. This means breaking it down into discrete elements, arranging these elements in relation to one another, and then reassembling these elements with the aid of a series of perceptual-motor and intuitive regulations" (Piaget and Inhelder 1967:55).

Among these regulations are the simple topological relations I discussed in Part I—proximity, separation, order, and so on. There are of course physical constraints on drawing. For example, Van Sommers (1984) found that right-handers, with few exceptions, prefer to make strokes down to the right rather than up to the left. He attributes this preference to body geometry, the actual biomechanical constraints of moving a pencil or pen. These biomechanical factors constrain the direction of scribbling and, combined with rhythmic repetition, produce the unordered figures we associate with the earliest drawing. It is not until the child breaks down these constraints and produces discrete actions that we can begin to speak of spatial *concepts*. "Thus it comes about that as soon as the rhythmic movement has been broken down into discrete elements, *the very fact of connecting or not connecting them together* results in relationships of proximity and separation, closure and openness, ordered succession and continuity" (Piaget and Inhelder 1967:67; emphasis mine). It is the act of connecting and the way of connecting that are the source of these topological notions. Relations such as proximity are the first to appear because they are the simplest way to break down and recombine the mechanical and rhythmic patterns of scribbling. More complex concepts arise through subsequent coordination of the simpler concepts.

Rhythmic motion and the constraints of body geometry are as applicable to stone knapping as they are to drawing. Even bashing two rocks together employs the rhythmic action of swinging and the body geometry of hands, wrists, forearms, shoulders, and so on, all of which constrain the trajectories of the blows. Spatial concepts arise through the interruption of this basic biomechanical action, the isolation of discrete motions from the general rhythm, and the connection of these discrete motions to one another. The artifacts in examples 1 and 2 required little more than the basic rhythmic action of repeated striking. The coordination was very rudimentary. The knapper need only have struck the cobbles in more or less the same places, an action that required some interruption of the basic rhythms of knapping and the connection of these discrete actions to one another.

Such an elementary notion may seem rudimentary to the point of absurdity. Nevertheless, it is the simplest possible organization of action, in stone knapping as well as in drawing, and is therefore a necessary first step in the intentional alteration of objects. Not only was it an unavoidable first step, it was necessarily the source of subsequent notions of space, which are nothing more nor less than coordinations of this initial relation. A chopper, for example, requires a notion of placing one trimming blow immediately adjacent to a previous one, indeed using a previous flake scar as a reference point. One must coordinate the more primitive notions of interrupted rhythm and nearness into a more directed order of action, namely the making of a pair. Furthermore, some choppers, at least, boast bifacial edges. Here the coordination includes adherence to a boundary (the edge), away from which the trimming blows have to be directed—again a more complicated separation and control of the discrete actions of knapping. The unifacial edges of examples 6a, 6b, and 6c add to this coordination the notion of sequence of flake scars. At first it may seem that nothing more than rhythmic flaking is necessary for such edges. After all, what could be simpler than to hold a cobble or flake and, by repeated rhythmic striking, produce a unifacial edge? Motor rhythms are just motor rhythms, however. There is no inherent direction or coordination. It is the concept in the maker's head, a conscious organization of action schemes, that supplies direction. For an even unifacial edge, the knapper had to place each trimming flake in relation to all of the others. This requires a concept that orders blows not just into pairs, but into longer sequences.

Stone knapping was not as premeditated and laborious as this may sound. The actual process required little reflection and no doubt took only a few seconds. Nevertheless, the striking of trimming flakes required concepts, as rudimentary as this might seem, and the first spatial concepts are tied to action. If the world had been simply perceived by hominids one day as a complex euclidean organization, then artifacts would have been more sophisticated right from the start. Their simplicity was not a matter of motor control. Artifacts from the earliest sites show fineness of hand. Early artifacts are crude because early hominids had not yet structured space in the way we so casually understand it.

The coordination required for proximity, separation, pairs, and sequences is well within the scope of preoperational reasoning. Even though I have described these topological notions in terms of simple and coordinated action schemes, I am not suggesting anything like a sensorimotor level of intelligence. These schemes were almost certainly internalized action schemes. We must assume that Oldowan tools were the result of intention, that is, made for some particular task at hand. Such intention requires projection of action into the future in the form of some internal representation. This representation is the primary characteristic that distinguishes preoperational reasoning from sensorimotor schemes. However, the internalized action schemes required for the manufacture of Oldowan tools were not very complex. It was unnecessary for the knapper to have considered more than one effect of his action at a time. Even in making the scraper—the most topologically sophisticated Oldowan tool—the knapper need only have attended to the placing of a trimming blow in relation to the previous ones of a perceivable sequence. That is, he only had to control one quality. This is typical of internalized action schemes, which can only consider one variable at a time. Nowhere among Oldowan artifacts do we find evidence for the simultaneous consideration of several variables. These artifacts could easily be the result of trial and error—knock off one or a few flakes, check the result, and if unsatisfactory, continue trimming. The reversible anticipation of operational intelligence was not necessary, and, because we can only assess minimum necessary competence, we must conclude that Oldowan stone knappers used preoperational reasoning.

It is difficult to reach a more precise characterization than this general one of preoperational intelligence. As described earlier, preoperational intelligence is often divided into two substages, symbolic and intuitive, distinguished primarily by the degree to which a child focuses potential action on himself. Some tasks, such as trial-and-error reversal of spatial order, are accomplished only in the second substage (see below). All of the spatial concepts identified for Oldowan hominids are found in the earlier substage of preoperational intelligence (Piaget and Inhelder 1967:80–92). Thus it cannot be argued that Oldowan hominids possessed a particularly advanced form of preoperational intelligence. Again, this is the *minimum* competence necessary for the tools.

Nothing in the archaeological record of the Oldowan argues against this assessment. Recently there has been much debate over the meaning of tools and animal bones found at Olduvai sites (Potts 1984; Binford 1985; Isaac 1984). Clearly, the hominids carried both stones and bones; clearly, they relied more on meat than do any of the modern great apes. But we do not know if they shared these things, or used "home bases." Indeed, current analysis argues against these conclusions. And even if we ultimately find them to be true, they are all well within the abilities of preoperational intelligence. Nothing about sharing or home base or meat eating requires operational intelligence. Indeed, the Oldowan industry as a whole corroborates the evidence of artifact geometry. When one examines entire collections of Oldowan tools, one finds a wide range of artifact sizes, amounts of trimming, and edge morphologies, but it is very difficult to subdivide the collections into classes and sub-classes. Much of the variation that does exist can be attributed to raw material. If hominids used preoperational reasoning this is just what we would expect, because preoperational thinking is incapable of creating classes as we usually understand them. No *a priori* classes and sub-classes existed in the heads of these hominids. For each specific task the hominid probably had a specific size and edge in mind, and chipped until he achieved that result—by trial and error. This kind of toolmaking would yield a range of forms with few, if any, perceivable modalities—which is just what we see in the Oldowan.

Implications

It is traditional to emphasize the human-like characteristics of these early hominids. I believe it is just as reasonable, however, to emphasize their ape-like characteristics. The archaeological record, for example, argues for preoperational intelligence, which is also typical of modern apes. There are several lines of evidence to support this contention, some of them dealing with spatial relations and some with linguistic ability.

Parker (1976), Redshaw (1978), and Chevalier-Skolnikoff (1976) have applied the Piagetian stage model to the ontogeny of infant gorillas. They have found that gorillas pass through the same sequence of sensorimotor substages as human infants, and achieve the most advanced level of sensorimotor intelligence. The only significant difference is that the gorilla does not apply the most complex action in its vocal behavior. In addition to corroborating the interspecific applicability of Piaget's model, these studies have demonstrated that in the domain of object manipulation, gorillas achieve at least the most advanced level of sensorimotor intelligence. No work has been done with apes applying specifically preoperational spatial concepts, but there are other results, interpretable in Piagetian terms, that argue for fully preoperational organizations.

Parker and Gibson (1979) have reviewed reports on various specific abilities of great apes. They assessed such actions as object manipulation, copying of geometric figures, and construction of collections. For example, apes do not employ true classification, and only attend to topological qualities when copying figures. Parker and Gibson concluded that the great apes displayed behavior typical of the symbolic substage (first substage) of the preoperational stage.

The above assessments were made on captive apes, and one could argue that such results do not reflect the organizational abilities naturally employed by great apes. Ethological studies, however, also supply evidence for preoperational spatial concepts. Chimpanzees, for example, modify natural objects for use as tools. In making termite "fishing poles" (van Lawick-Goodall 1970; Teleki 1974) and "ant-dipping sticks" (McGrew 1974), the chimps select appropriate grass stems or branches and strip off leaves and twigs. Such stripping requires some notion of end result (especially when the modification is done away from the intended termite mound) and some procedure for achieving it. The minimum procedure is preoperational trial and error. Such tasks are not directly comparable to stone knapping because the chimps need not place elements in specific relation to one another, but need merely remove perceived hindrances. Nevertheless, this toolmaking behavior indicates that chimpanzees naturally employ preoperational organization to solve problems.

Recent studies in ape language acquisition demonstrate conclusively that chimpanzees and gorillas have representational ability (Premack 1976a, 1976b; Terrace et al. 1979). Their use of non-iconic symbols can be explained in no other way. There remains considerable controversy over whether their use of symbols also qualifies as language, but this is not directly relevant to our discussion. It is the ability to represent, especially to represent action within thought, that distinguishes preoperational intelligence from sensorimotor intelligence. Chimpanzees and gorillas symbolize about action through verbs and simple causal relations (Premack 1976a). They are, therefore, internalizing action, and this is preoperational intelligence. Of course, none of the animal behavior studies that employ Piagetian theory would argue that ape behavior is equivalent to that of human children. There are obvious differences. Nor would I argue that Oldowan hominids were like human children. I am only arguing that similar principles of organization are and were used by all of them.

In sum, it appears that modern apes have at least preoperational intelligence. Moreover, they use this kind of intelligence in making tools. They even carry certain kinds of hammers from place to place to use as "nutting stones" (Boesch and Boesch 1984). They do not make stone tools like those of the Oldowan, but their lack of a lithic technology appears not to result from any cognitive restrictions.

It seems, then, that Oldowan hominids were not yet beyond the range of ape behavior. What implications does this conclusion have for our understanding of human evolution? There are two ways to approach this question. We can assume that the Piagetian assessment of minimum competence is wrong and underrepresents Oldowan intelligence, or we can assume that the assessment is essentially correct. The implications of these assumptions are rather different, but neither corresponds to a traditional view.

It is possible that this assessment of minimum competence has undervalued hominid intelligence. It is, admittedly, based on a narrow range of behavior and, even from a Piagetian perspective, might be unrepresentative of other behaviors. It may be that Oldowan hominids used their most sophisticated organizational abilities in such domains as foraging, social relations, or communication, but used only simple organizations in the actual manufacture of tools. The archaeological record does not rule out this possibility, but neither does it support it. Nothing in the archaeological evidence for foraging demands organizational abilities beyond those of the preoperational stage. This leaves "invisible" behaviors such as social organization and language. It is certainly possible that selection for intelligence resides in social behavior rather than in technology. Indeed, there is growing evidence for this in primate studies (e.g., Humphrey 1976). In other words, if this assessment is wrong, and the hominids were in fact more intelligent than their tools suggest, then toolmaking and tool use were not factors in the early evolution of human intelligence. Of course, such a possibility runs counter to the "tools makyth man" bias of many archaeologists.

It is, I suppose, more parsimonious to accept the archaeological evidence as an accurate reflection of the overall intelligence of these hominids. If the assessment is accurate, then the evolution of a uniquely hominid intelligence had not occurred by Oldowan times. However, the basic hominid morphology of upright posture had been attained by 3.5 million years ago (Johanson and White 1979). This suggests that selection for a complex organizing intelligence was not part of the original hominid adaptation. For several million years hominids did not rely on some special cleverness not possessed by other hominoids. Selection for human-like intelligence appears not to have been significant until after the Oldowan.

The Intelligence of Early Acheulean Hominids

Sometime around one-and-a-half million years ago, Oldowan assemblages in East Africa were replaced by assemblages that included large, bifacially trimmed tools, often made on large flakes. This technological development is striking and is accorded considerable importance in descriptions of early prehistory. Paradoxically, however, archaeologists know less about the behavior of these stone knappers than about the makers of Oldowan tools. We simply do not have the large, relatively well-preserved sites that are known for the earlier period. Perhaps the good record for Oldowan hominids is simply serendipity, or perhaps there was a significant change in typical living arrangements. Whatever the case, we know very little about the day-to-day activities of these early biface-using hominids. We do have several sites and several good collections of tools, however, and these allow us to make assessments of the technology alone, including assessments of spatial concepts.

As we saw in Part I, two spatial concepts appear about 1.5 million years ago that are unknown in the Oldowan: the notion of interval and the notion of reversal (symmetry). Both of these appear to have played a role in building a notion of the artifact as a whole, though the visualized whole was at best a two-dimensional shape.

Piaget's stage scheme is not very helpful here. None of these spatial concepts requires the reversibility and conservation of operational intelligence, so the minimum necessary competence is still preoperational. Yet intuitively there appears to be quite a difference between the competence required for these tools and that required for Oldowan tools. Part of the problem is that the preoperational stage is the least well-defined stage of Piaget's scheme, and, by Piaget's own admission, encompasses a continuum of development (Piaget 1960, 1972). The beginning is fairly well marked by the advent of representation and the end is fairly well marked by the acquisition of operations, but distinguishing between "early" and "late" preoperations is not a straightforward task. Preoperational intelligence has often been divided into two substages, "symbolic" and "intuitive," distinguished primarily by the degree to which a child focuses action on himself (see above, p. 75). This distinction is rather subtle, and relies largely on dialogues with children, a useless technique in prehistory. Some spatial tasks are accomplished only during the second substage. The one relevant spatial concept is the ability to reverse a spatial order. If we wish to hang an assessment on a very thin thread, and argue that the crude symmetry of early bifaces is the product of such trial-and-error reversals of spatial order, then we can put these hominids in the substage of intuitive preoperations. But this is a very thin thread indeed, and, moreover, such an assessment seems a rather sterile accomplishment. I find it more enlightening to look at the kind of development that occurs during the preoperational stage, and use this more dynamic picture to help us understand the early biface makers.

The key concept here is decentration. Just as an infant's initial action schemes are tied directly to immediate perception (so that, for example, when a toy is hidden the infant ceases grasping for it), the initial representations of preoperational thought are tied to the perceptions (including viewpoints!) and potential action of the child himself. Piaget terms this "egocentric." During the course of the preoperational stage, thought frees itself from the focus on ego and comes to understand and expect relations between independent objects, persons, and so on (Piaget 1960, 1972). When this understanding can logically exclude errors, the operational stage has been reached. Many of the differences we see between spatial concepts of the early Acheulean and those of the Oldowan suggest a relative decentration. Simple Oldowan concepts such as proximity and order could be the result of ego-centered preoperations. Indeed, that is the minimum competence. The concept of whole and the shapes true of bifaces suggest, on the other hand, a notion of artifact apart from the immediate task at hand. The artifact appears to have existed independent of the action and thought of ego, and this is relative decentration.

Corroborating this assessment is the presence, for the first time, of what can legitimately be called "classes" of artifacts. It is relatively easy for an archaeologist to recognize the handaxes and cleavers in these early biface assemblages. This suggests some kind of a standard that was shared, which in turn suggests that stone knappers attended to

shapes produced by others. In addition, by the end of the preoperational stage children can produce rudimentary classes defined by single qualities (Piaget 1972). The single distinction of "pointed" vs. "bit-
ted" (the transverse, untrimmed end of a cleaver) would be sufficient
to encompass the handaxe-cleaver distinction that we do see in the
early biface industries.

In sum, despite the relative poverty of evidence, there do appear to
be differences between Oldowan and early Acheulean assemblages
that are consistent with a Piagetian view of intellectual development.
In particular, the preoperational concepts of these stone knappers
show greater decentration and are, therefore, further along the road
to operational thought.

Implications

If accurate, this assessment places the intelligence of these early
Acheulean hominids beyond the range of modern apes. Though the
evidence is equivocal, almost all relevant ape behavior falls within the
earlier substage of preoperational intelligence (Parker and Gibson
1979:369). In other respects as well, the tools of these hominids differ
from those of apes, who invariably manufacture termiting sticks and
ant-fishing sticks in an *ad hoc* manner, with no evidence of standard-
ization like that true for early bifaces (Wynn 1989). It appears, then,
that these hominids had taken a step in the direction of humanness
and away from apeness, and that a more powerful intelligence was
part of the process. Unfortunately, the lack of evidence for other
kinds of behavior, subsistence for example, makes it impossible to
know whether technology was a leading element in this evolution or
simply reflected selection for intelligence in other realms.

The Intelligence of Later Acheulean Hominids

The most straightforward, and perhaps the most unexpected, conclusion of this Piagetian analysis is that hominids had achieved operational intelligence by 300,000 years ago, and perhaps earlier. The
conclusion is straightforward because it is supported by topological,
projective, and euclidean concepts that were clearly and repeatedly
used in the making of stone tools. It is unexpected because it places
an essentially modern intelligence much earlier than the time of the
first appearance of hominids with completely modern anatomy, that
is, *Homo sapiens sapiens*.

The notion of analysis and synthesis, exemplified by the minimally
trimmed Isimila bifaces, requires the conception of the object as an
inclusive whole, one that is made up of coordinated parts. In making

a minimally trimmed biface (that in Figure 7, for example) the knapper needed first to conceive of the shape in terms of *potential* trimming, and then he had to choose which of the trimming was essential
and which superfluous or even detrimental to the intended result.
This process of analysis and synthesis, however quickly it probably
occurred, required reversibility and pre-correction of errors. Trial-
and-error trimming could only have attained the imagined shape by
trimming and checking, trimming and checking, until the intended
shape was approximated, usually by contiguous flaking and rarely
through a minimum amount of work. In other words, this one topological concept *alone* argues for the use of operations by 300,000 years
ago. Ironically, it is not the "fine" artifacts but the relatively simple
ones that make the case for analysis and synthesis. But it is the fine,
extensively trimmed artifacts that provide evidence for projective and
euclidean spatial operations.

Projective concepts provide the two most persuasive lines of evidence. We saw earlier how important the acquisition of perspective
was to the development of spatial concepts. Two of the projective notions used by Isimila hominids required operational intelligence: the
notion of straight edges and the notion of regular cross sections.

In order to conceive of and execute a straight line, an individual
must be able to relate all of the points to a stable point of view. This
relation is reversible in the Piagetian sense. Each point must be related to all of the other points *and* to a stable viewpoint. If point D is
in line with points C and B, and C and B are in line with A, then D is
also, by necessity, in line with A. This concept, which Piaget terms
operational "qualitative displacement," is an organizational principle
used in arranging any series, by size for example (A<B<C<D). It is
also equivalent to mathematical transitivity. As we saw in Part I, there
are arguably straight edges on several of the Isimila artifacts, edges
that were extensively trimmed and whose shape was clearly intentional. Such edges required a stable point of view and the reversible
relation of "in line." Such reversibility within an organizational principle is typical of operational intelligence.

More telling than straight edges, which are admittedly uncommon,
are the regular cross sections of many of the Isimila bifaces. Trial-
and-error flaking, the only kind of planning available to preoperational thought, is simply inadequate for the task of conceiving and
executing such cross sections. Many of the bifaces have a virtual infinity of regular cross sections—this is one of the characteristics that
make them so attractive. To make such an artifact by trial and error,
controlling one variable at a time, the knapper could check and alter
one visible cross section but could not, at the same time, control the

effect of his action on other cross sections. He could, of course, then check and alter another, and in the process risk ruining the one he had already finished. Such a hit-and-miss process could, after much trimming, achieve a vaguely regular solid, but this would be almost pure serendipity. To be sure of the intended result—and the Isimila bifaces argue for considerable confidence—the knapper needed to be able to pre-correct errors. During trimming, the modification of the surface to regularize the shape of the cross section from one point of view could not be allowed to ruin other cross sections, most of which could not be directly observed. These unobservable cross sections must have been purely mental constructs.

For such cross sections, pre-correction relies upon what Piaget terms "spatio-temporal substitution." This is the understanding of the potential interchangeability of points of view. An example of such interchangeability is the ability to recognize familiar landmarks when they are approached from a new direction. One must rearrange certain familiar attributes of the object into a new *but equivalent* configuration (reverse left-right order, for example) and must also substitute new attributes for familiar ones that are no longer visible. The result is an image of the same whole—the landmark—but one that has been constructed in quite a different manner. Such arranging and rearranging requires the ability to return to a starting point in thought. "In the case of operations such as joining neighboring parts of an object $(A + A' = B; B + B' = C$, etc.) the reverse projective operation involves suppressing one element $(B-A' = A$, etc.) which can no longer be seen through being hidden by another object acting as a screen. This subtractive operation expresses a section . . ." (Piaget and Inhelder 1967:469). As is unfortunately often the case, Piaget's prose is far from lucid. What is important is that in combining elements to create a cross section, one must use the same organizing tools, addition and subtraction for example, that one would use in building a classification. Equivalency is also an element of formal classification; the same class can be subdivided in different ways $(A_1 + A_1' = A_2 + A_2' = B)$ but each conserves the original class. In the same way, one perspective of a regular cross section conserves the shape in a manner equivalent to that of another section. In the case of cross sections it is a matter of constantly monitoring many equivalent viewpoints, some visible, most not. It simply cannot be done with preoperational trial-and-error plans.

The final spatial concept that argues for operational thought is congruency. The Isimila bifaces are symmetrical in more than one dimension. Moreover, the shape that is reversed is often a virtual duplicate, that is, a congruency. Symmetry alone, in the sense of mirroring, is not necessarily euclidean, but a congruent symmetry is. And this requires some abstract notion of measurement and a general spatial framework in which it applies. Such a frame of measured distance can be used to create a "substitute" for a shape which can be reversed in thought and used as a model controlling the mirrored shape. Because the frame is arbitrary, it must be constructed in thought—by spatio-temporal substitution—and every point in one figure must be reversed, precisely, in its mirror. Such feats are again beyond the scope of preoperations.

I find this symmetry argument for operations to be the weakest of the four. The assumption of congruency seems shaky. If it stood alone, I would hesitate to argue for operational thought at 300,000 years ago. However, the evidence from the other spatial concepts, especially analysis and synthesis and spatio-temporal substitution, is to me so convincing that I see the symmetry as corroborative.

In sum, the geometry of Isimila bifaces argues convincingly that Isimila hominids used operational thinking in their spatial concepts by 300,000 years ago. These complex geometric relationships cannot have been accidentally imposed, and preoperational intelligence is simply insufficient for their conception and execution.

Implications

To conclude that hominids employed operational intelligence 300,000 years ago is to conclude that hominids possessed an essentially modern intelligence by this relatively early date. I am here using operational intelligence *sensu latu*, for the moment ignoring the distinction between concrete and formal operations, which I will discuss in the next section. Traditionally, students of human evolution have assumed that modern intelligence evolved hand in hand with modern anatomy, that is, with the appearance of *Homo sapiens sapiens*. The Piagetian analysis suggests that very early *Homo sapiens* were as intelligent, in the main, as later *Homo sapiens*. They, too, used the powerful organizing principles of reversibility, conservation, transitivity, precorrection of errors, and so on. Of course, if we put 300,000 years into the perspective of all of human evolution, it is in fact relatively late, marking at most the last 15 percent, and so this conclusion is not really surprising, especially given the early dates for some *Homo sapiens* fossils (Jelinek 1980).

The structural nature of Piaget's theory invites us to extend our conclusions from the realm of spatial concepts to all of intelligence. But here we run into one of the most controversial aspects of the theory. How general is it? If a hominid used transitivity in technology, must he also have used it in kinship? In psychological research, Piaget's scheme of stages has held up reasonably well within specific domains (Siegler and Richards 1982), such as spatial concepts. It is when the net is thrown wide that failures in correlation appear. As a consequence, I believe it safe to conclude that these hominids used operations in spatial tasks like technology and geography (mapping, and so on) and probably in organizing other physical phenomena. I do not think it perfectly safe to extend these abilities to other domains of behavior. I think this is a reasonable supposition, but we may never know. Certainly, to say that these hominids used operational intelligence tells us nothing about their content of mind, their actual knowledge—whether or not they had a language with formal grammar, or a numbering system, or a seasonal pattern of movement. We only know that their organizing ability and principles of problem solving were essentially modern.

A final point concerns the role of technology in the evolution of intelligence. If we consider range of tool types, there is very little difference between the early and later Acheulean. Both have bifaces, discoids, spheroids, and a range of small tools made on flakes, including unifacial scrapers and tools with trimmed projections. Neither presents the distinctly partitioned set of easily recognizable types or classes of flake tools that is characteristic of later periods and often interpreted as reflecting technological specialization. Indeed, there is no obvious difference between the tasks that could be performed by early and later Acheulean tools. However, when we compare the spatial concepts required for the two, there is a dramatic difference that indicates that the later hominids were significantly more intelligent. If there was no obvious correlation between a change in technology, in the guise of a change in tasks performed, and a change in intelligence, it is difficult to argue that one drives the other. There is always the chance that we are missing some important invisible component of technology, but as the evidence stands we cannot argue for a central role for technology in the evolution of intelligence between 1.5 million years ago and 300,000 years ago. If not tools, what? The most likely candidates appear to be complex social organizations and semiotic behavior, especially language. Neither is likely to be clearly manifested in tools.

After the Acheulean

In the previous section I argued that an essentially modern intelligence was a hominid characteristic by 300,000 years ago. By "essentially modern" I mean operational intelligence in the broad sense. I have so far intentionally avoided discussion of Piaget's distinction between concrete and formal operations. Is it not probable that the spatial operations that I have identified at 300,000 years ago reflect only an ability in concrete operations, and that hominids achieved the stage of formal operations at a later date, perhaps only relatively recently? Unfortunately, the question of the formal operational stage is a truly difficult one. First of all, it is almost impossible to recognize in the archaeological record. Second, it may not be a "real" stage at all, but rather a style of reasoning learned in Western schools.

The very nature of formal operational intelligence makes it virtually invisible archaeologically. Recall that formal operations organize hypothetical entities and relationships of various kinds. These are of course invisible. Formal operations also coordinate two kinds of reversibility—inversion and reciprocity—making for "foolproof" plans. But such coordination cannot be recognized in the products of behavior. In the example of the balance used earlier (p. 77), both concrete and formal operational thinkers can balance the scale successfully. Their strategies may differ slightly, but the archaeologist would find only the balanced scale, not the strategies.

The spatial concepts described in this book are all the stuff of concrete operations. Projective, topological, and euclidean spaces are all "real" spaces in the sense that they organize tangible things and perspectives. It is of course possible to speculate about multi-dimensional spaces and hypothetical geometries, but one cannot, as far as I know, use them to arrange objects. The everyday world is organized by concrete operations, and it is the everyday world that archaeologists find most often. The consequence of all of this is that we cannot use artifacts and spatial concepts to argue for the evolution of formal operations.

This conclusion removes from consideration two of archaeologists' favorite markers of prehistoric cleverness—Levallois technique and prismatic core technique. In the former, the knapper "pre-forms" the core in order to control the shape of one final flake. Many see this "pre-forming" and "seeing the flake in the core" as requiring more intelligence than that needed for mere handaxes. This is a common-sense conclusion. From a Piagetian perspective, Levallois technique requires the topological operation of analysis and synthesis or, more simply, pre-correction of errors. But it does not require the spatio-temporal substitution or symmetry relations of handaxes, and so, in this sense, is less sophisticated than handaxes. I am not arguing that Levallois does not require great skill, but skill is not the same as intelligence. Similarly, prismatic blade cores require concrete operations (barely!) but certainly do not argue for a more powerful intelligence than do handaxes. They were an important invention but do not represent a leap in intelligence.

In order to document the appearance of formal operations, one must turn to *interpretations* of the palaeolithic, thereby removing the analysis one giant step away from the evidence itself. I have considered many of these elsewhere (Wynn 1986) but, as this is a book on spatial concepts, I will limit myself here to a brief discussion of the one possible bit of evidence for palaeolithic formal operations— Upper Palaeolithic parietal art.

It is only in the realm of ritual that we find the glimmerings of organizations beyond the scope of concrete operations. Of course, even modest interpretations of palaeolithic ritual behavior are controversial, and Leroi-Gourhan's (1967), the one I will use, is not modest. It is an ambitious hypothesis that argues for a rather specific symbolic system centered on male-female dualism. I am not so much interested in his ultimate conclusions as I am in the patterns he has documented to support them. These consist of associations and repetitions in Franco-Cantabrian cave art, associations and repetitions that suggest something fascinating about the prehistoric classification system. In all of the caves examined by Leroi-Gourhan, 91 percent of the painted bison are located in the central portion of the caves. In addition, 64 percent of these bison are associated with horses. Certain geometric "signs" are common elements of painted panels, and one category of these signs—"wide" signs consisting of rectangles, squares, and so on—dominates the central portions of the caves. In other words, Leroi-Gourhan has documented a consistently repeated association of bison, horses, wide geometric signs, and cave topography in Upper Palaeolithic art. This association was also noticed, independently, by Laming-Emperaire (Leroi-Gourhan 1967 : 10), a fact that suggests it is not all in Leroi-Gourhan's imagination.

If bison, horses, and "wide signs" do represent a coherent association of symbolic value, then they represent a rather abstract form of classification, one whose shared qualities are certainly not of the real world. Concrete operational classification groups members based on tangible similarities, but not on hypothetical commonalities (Piaget 1969). One could argue that bison and horses constitute a class defined by tangible similarities (large, furry, animal) but this does not appear to be what the Magdalenian painters had in mind. Bison and horses share something with wide signs as well, something that allows all of them to be grouped together into one class. The animals, signs, and positions were grouped according to some common abstract feature (whether or not this is "femaleness" is irrelevant), and not according to a tangible similarity. This requires formal operations, at

least as Piaget generally defined them. But this conclusion should sur-
prise no one. It places formal operational intelligence 16,000 years
ago, which, from a Stone Age perspective, is almost the present.

A search for formal operations in the palaeolithic may, in fact, be
pointless. They are not only elusive in prehistory, they are elusive in
the modern world. "The very few cross-cultural studies that have included tasks of the formal operational stage have found very little
evidence of formal operational performance" (Dasen and Herron
1981:332). Indeed, only one-half of high school and college students
perform the "balance" task using formal operations (Siegler and Richards 1982:917). Concrete operations, on the other hand, appear to
be universal. The absence of formal operations is thought-provoking,
especially given the complex behaviors produced by so-called primitive peoples. Micronesian sailors can travel hundreds of miles between tiny atolls using an elaborate system of sidereal navigation,
ocean currents, knowledge of birds, and so on, and yet do not perform well on Piagetian tasks (Gladwin 1970). This failure may reflect
lack of experience rather than of competence. Balancing a scale is
familiar and relevant to Swiss high school students (half of them, any-
way!) but unfamiliar to a Micronesian sailor. Indeed, evidence seems
to indicate that formal operations are a "style" of thinking one learns
in Western education (Rogoff 1981; Scinto 1984). This makes formal
operations no less useful, but it does seriously challenge their status
as a stage of intellectual development.

In sum, there is no reason to believe that a stage of "formal" operations marks the end of the phylogenetic sequence. The archaeological
record argues for no significant developments in *competence* after
300,000 years ago. Even if one accepts the evidence from parietal art
as evidence for formal operations, the difference between this kind of
reasoning and that documented for the Acheulean is no greater than
that which we can document between Swiss high school students and
Micronesian sailors. And this seems not to be difference in competence at all.

Summary and Conclusions

For the next few paragraphs I would once again like to leave behind
careful analysis and speculate on larger implications. It is fine to argue
that Oldowan hominids had preoperational intelligence, but how
does this fit into our understanding of human evolution? What has
the Piagetian analysis given us beyond sterile description?

The Piagetian assessment of the Oldowan corroborates recent research that emphasizes the apelike characteristics of these early homi-

nids. As we have seen, the spatial concepts used to make Oldowan tools are rudimentary, well within the criteria for early preoperational thinking and, as a consequence, well within the conceptual abilities of modern apes. These hominids could certainly project action into the future, much as chimpanzees anticipate termiting, but they would have been incapable of complex contingency plans. They could envision a goal, but could only approach the goal by trial and error. Of course, successful procedures could be learned by memorization of rote routines, in effect sensorimotor schemes, but these are not very flexible. Trial and error provides a kind of flexibility in behavior but it is relatively slow, cumbersome, and occasionally even dangerous. Moreover, if in fact the thinking of these hominids was characteristic of *early* preoperations, then their behavior was largely focused on ego (How do *I* relate to you? How can *I* obtain that desired food item?). Such thinking does not encompass social concepts, such as kinship, that present relationships that do not include ego directly. Again, this is much like the social systems of non-human primates, which are determined largely by one-on-one (ego + one) relationships. In addition, and I suspect this will be a controversial statement, such thinking would preclude complex divisions of labor based on sharing, with *planned* separations and recongregations. Foraging that used early preoperational thinking would be unlike anything we know of modern hunters and gatherers. But it would be very much like that which we know for modern apes. If we had a time machine, we would probably want to study Oldowan hominids in much the same way as ethologists study apes, and not as ethnographers study the !Kung San.

The above interpretation presumes that the assessment of minimum necessary competence is reliable. There is, in this case, a very real possibility that it underrepresents Oldowan intelligence. After all, there is a demonstrable difference in brain size and shape between Oldowan hominids (assuming early *Homo*) and modern apes (Holloway 1983), a difference that suggests a significant behavioral difference of some sort. It is unfortunate that we cannot yet argue from brain shape to behavior. For the latter we must still rely on archaeology, and, as we have seen, archaeology does not yet argue for a super-ape two million years ago.

By 1.2 million years ago, however, we do have evidence of something more sophisticated. Even though we have little direct evidence other than stone tools, the tools suggest that the hominids could organize an *external*, non-ego-centered world in a coherent fashion. There must have been a concept of artifact as separate from ego's action, and, more important, this concept must have included a *shared* community *standard*. In order for several hominids to have manufactured tools with the same shape, they must have shared some idea about what was appropriate and what was not. This is especially true when, as in the case of the biface, there is no overriding functional reason for the shape, which is essentially arbitrary. It would be difficult to overemphasize this development. It is a prerequisite to culture as we know it. I do not mean that these hominids had a modern culture; they almost certainly did not. But, perhaps for the first time, we can talk about a hominoid's behavior in terms of shared, arbitrary standards. There is no reason to suppose that such a shared, external world extended only to tools. It could well have included kinship (though not complex systems) and long-range, *planned* foraging. In this sense, the earlier Oldowan was not a beginning, but an end. The first *uniquely* hominid culture began only with the arrival of the biface makers.

Sometime in the next one million years, a milestone was reached. By 300,000 years ago hominids were using operational thinking, with all of its organizational power. Once again I must emphasize that this does not mean that culture was modern. But it does mean that these hominids, presumably late *Homo erectus* or early *Homo sapiens*, were capable of contingency planning, kinship based on true classification, concepts of number and notation, and so on. Not only could they operate in a world that existed apart from their own action, they could anticipate and take into account the obstacles that that world, natural or social, could present. I do not think we would find them brutish or dim-witted, though we certainly would not feel at home in their culture.

At the present state of our knowledge of the early Stone Age, we can only speculate about how and why the evolution from preoperational to operational thinking occurred. Selection for intelligence does not appear to have been closely tied to stone tools, whose shape (not refinement) and range of types remained more or less constant for one million years. Over the same period, however, intelligence clearly evolved. It may have been tied to complex foraging strategies such as large mammal hunting, though the evidence for this is controversial (see Binford 1985) and its implications for intelligence unclear. More likely, intelligence was tied to social and symbolic behavior. Recent research on non-human primates (for example, Byrne and Whiten 1988) suggests that social behaviors such as deception present more complex problems to solve than does foraging, and that primate intelligence is primarily a social intelligence. One must extend such social intelligence to early hominids, especially since it is obviously a characteristic of modern human behavior as well. It is as easy to envision the need for social solutions to evolutionary problems as it is to envision the need for technological solutions to them. When one adds complex symbolic systems such as language to complex social systems, the result is an evolutionary scenario of such potential complexity that simple tool behavior pales in comparison.

The period between 1.5 million years ago and 300,000 years ago was a critical one in human evolution. It seems likely to me that it was during this period that human social and symbolic systems evolved in complexity far beyond any known for apes, and that selection for intelligence was an essential component. Some aspects of tool morphology may reflect this development, and may even have played a role (Wynn 1989), but tools do not seem to have been leading elements. But whatever the causes, by 300,000 years ago hominid reasoning ability had become essentially modern.

References

Atran, S. (1982). "Constraints on a Theory of Hominid Tool-making Behavior." *L'Homme* 22(2), 35–68.

Binford, L. (1985). "Human Ancestors: Changing Views of Their Behavior." *Journal of Anthropological Archaeology* 4, 292–327.

Boesch, C., and H. Boesch (1984). "Mental Map in Wild Chimpanzees: An Analysis of Hammer Transports for Nut Cracking." *Primates* 25(2), 160–70.

Bordes, F. (1968). *The Old Stone Age*. New York: McGraw Hill.

Byrne, R., and A. Whiten (eds.) (1988). *Machiavellian Intelligence: Social Expertise and the Evolution of Intellect in Monkeys, Apes, and Humans*. Oxford: Oxford University Press.

Chavaillon, J., N. Chavaillon, R. Hours, and M. Piperno (1979). "From the Oldowan to the Middle Stone Age at Melka-Kunture (Ethiopia). Understanding Cultural Changes." *Quaternaria* 21, 87–114.

Chevalier-Skolnikoff, S. (1976). "The Ontogeny of Primate Intelligence and Its Implications for Communicative Potential." In *Origins and Evolution of Language and Speech*, ed. S. Harnad, D. Steklis, and J. Lancaster. Annals of the New York Academy of Sciences 280, 173–211.

Chinn, W. G., and N. E. Steenrud (1966). *First Concepts of Topology*. New York: Random House.

Clark, J. D., and H. Kurashina. (1979). "Hominid Occupation of the East-central Highlands of Ethiopia in the Plio-Pleistocene." *Nature* 282, 33–39.

Cole, G. H., and M. R. Kleindienst (1974). "Further Reflections on the Isimila Acheulian." *Quaternary Research* 4, 346–55.

Dasen, P., and A. Herron (1981). "Cross-cultural Tests of Piaget's Theory." In *Handbook of Cross-Cultural Psychology, Vol. 4: Developmental Psychology*, ed. H. Triandis and A. Herron, pp. 295–341. Boston: Allyn and Bacon.

Dennell, R. (1983). *European Economic Prehistory*. London: Academic Press.

Gladwin, T. (1970). *East is a Big Bird*. Cambridge, Mass.: Harvard University Press.

Gould, S. (1977). *Ontogeny and Phylogeny*. Cambridge, Mass.: Harvard University Press.

Hansen, C. L., and C. M. Keller (1971). "Environment and Activity Pattern-
ing at Isimila Korongo, Iringa District, Tanzania: A Preliminary Report."
American Anthropologist 73(5), 1202–11.

Hay, R. (1976). *The Geology of Olduvai Gorge.* Berkeley: University of
California.

Holloway, R. L. (1981). "Cultural Symbols and Brain Evolution: A Synthesis."
Dialectical Anthropology 5:287–303.

——— (1983). "Human Brain Evolution: A Search for Units, Models and
Synthesis." *Canadian Journal of Anthropology* 3(2), 215–30.

Howell, F. C., G. H. Cole, and M. R. Kleindienst (1962). "Isimila, an Acheulian Occupation Site in the Iringa Highlands, Southern Highlands Prov-
ince, Tanganyika." *Actes du IV⁴ Congrès Panafricain de Préhistoire et de
l'Etude du Quaternaire*, ed. G. Mortelmans and J. Nenquin. Annales Musée
de l'Afrique Centrale, Série in 8⁴, Sciences Humaines 40, 43–80.

Howell, F. C., G. H. Cole, M. R. Kleindienst, B. J. Szabo, and K. P. Oakley
(1972). "Uranium-series Dating of Bone from the Isimila Prehistoric Site,
Tanzania." *Nature* 237, 51–52.

Humphrey, N. K. (1976). "The Social Function of Intellect." In *Growing Points
in Ethology*, ed. P. P. G. Bateson and R. A. Hinde, pp. 303–17. Cambridge: Cambridge University Press.

Inhelder, B., J. Piaget, and A. Szeminksa (1960). *The Child's Conception of Geometry*, trans. A. Lunzer. London: Routledge and Kegan Paul.

Isaac, G. L. (1967). "The Stratigraphy of the Peninj Group—Early Middle
Pleistocene Formations West of Lake Natron, Tanzania." In *Background
to Evolution in Africa*, ed. W. Bishop and J. Clark. Chicago: University of
Chicago Press.

——— (1976a). "Plio-Pleistocene Artifact Assemblages from East Rudolf,
Kenya." In *Earliest Man and Environments in the Lake Rudolf Basin*, ed. Y.
Coppens, F. C. Howell, G. Isaac, and R. Leakey, pp. 552–64. Chicago:
University of Chicago Press.

——— (1976b). "Stratigraphy and Cultural Patterns in East Africa." In *After
the Australo-pithecines*, ed. K. Butzer and G. Isaac. The Hague: Mouton.

——— (1977). *Olorgesailie.* Chicago: University of Chicago Press.

——— (1984). "The Archaeology of Human Origins: Studies of the Lower
Pleistocene in East Africa 1971–1981." *Advances in World Archaeology* 3,
1–86.

———, and G. Curtis (1974). "The Age of Early Acheulian Industries in East
Africa—New Evidence from the Peninj Group, Tanzania." *Nature* 294,
624–27.

Jelinck, J. (1980). "European *Homo erectus* and the Origin of *Homo sapiens*." In
Current Argument on Early Man, ed. L. Konigsson, pp. 137–44. Oxford:
Pergamon Press.

Johanson, D., and T. White (1979). "A Systematic Assessment of Early Afri-
can Hominids." *Science* 203, 321–30.

Jones, P. R. (1981). "Experimental Implement Manufacture and Use: A Case

Study from Olduvai Gorge, Tanzania." In *The Emergence of Man*, ed. J. Young, E. Jope, and K. Oakley, pp. 189–95. London: The Royal Society and the British Academy.

Konkle, G. (1974). *Shapes and Perceptions: An Intuitive Approach to Geometry.* Boston: Prindle, Weber & Schmidt.

Leakey, M. (1971). *Olduvai Gorge*, vol. 3. Cambridge: Cambridge University Press.

Leroi-Gourhan, A. (1967). *Treasures of Prehistoric Art*, trans. N. Guterman. New York: Abrams.

Littleton, C. S. (1967). *The New Comparative Mythology*. Los Angeles: University of California Press.

McGrew, W. C. (1974). "Tool Use by Wild Chimpanzees in Feeding upon Driver Ants." *Journal of Human Evolution* 3, 501–8.

Merrick, H., and J. Merrick (1976). "Archaeological Occurrences of Lower Pleistocene Age from the Shungura Formation." In *Earliest Man and Environments in the Lake Rudolf Basin*, ed. Y. Coppens, F. C. Howell, G. Isaac, and R. Leakey, pp. 574–84. Chicago: University of Chicago Press.

Parker, S. (1976). "A Comparative Longitudinal Study of Sensorimotor Development in a Macaque, a Gorilla, and a Human Infant from a Piagetian Perspective." Paper presented at the Animal Behavior Society Conference, Boulder, Colorado.

——, and K. Gibson (1979). "A Developmental Model for the Evolution of Language and Intelligence in Early Hominids." *The Behavioral and Brain Sciences* 2, 367–408.

Piaget, J. (1960). *The Psychology of Intelligence*, trans. M. Piercy and D. Berlyne. Totowa, N.J.: Littlefield, Adams and Co.

—— (1969). "Problems of Genetic Psychology." In *Six Psychological Studies*, trans. A. Tenzer. New York: Vintage Press.

—— (1970). *Genetic Epistemology*, trans. E. Duckworth. New York: Harper.

—— (1971). *Psychology and Epistemology*, trans. A. Rosin. New York: Viking Press.

—— (1972). *The Principles of Genetic Epistemology*, trans. W. Mays. London: Kegan Paul.

—— (1973) *The Child and Reality*, trans. A. Rosin. New York: Grossman.

—— (1974). *Biology and Knowledge*, trans. B. Walsh. Chicago: University of Chicago Press.

——, and B. Inhelder (1967). *The Child's Conception of Space*, trans. F. Langlon and J. Lunzer. New York: Norton.

——, and B. Inhelder (1969). *The Psychology of the Child*. New York: Harper.

Potts, R. (1984). "Home Base and Early Hominids." *American Scientist* 72, 338–47.

Premack, D. (1976a). *Intelligence in Ape and Man*. Hillsdale, N.J.: Lawrence Erlbaum.

—— (1976b). "Mechanisms of Intelligence: Preconditions for Language." In *Origins and Evolution of Language and Speech*, ed. S. Harnad, H. Steklis, and J. Lancaster. *Annals of the New York Academy of Sciences* 280, 544–61.

Redshaw, M. (1978). "Cognitive Development in Human and Gorilla Infants." *Journal of Human Evolution* 7, 133–41.

Rightmire, G. P. (1981). "Stasis in the Evolution of *Homo erectus*." *Paleobiology* 7, 200–215.

Rogoff, B. (1981). "Schooling and the Development of Cognitive Skills." In *Handbook of Cross-Cultural Psychology, Vol. 4: Developmental Psychology*, ed. H. Triandis and A. Herron, pp. 233–94. Boston: Allyn and Bacon.

Scinto, L. (1984). "The Architectonics of Texts Produced by Children and the Development of Higher Cognitive Functions." *Discourse Processes* 7, 371–418.

Siegler, R. S., and D. Richards (1982). "The Development of Intelligence." In *Handbook of Human Intelligence*, ed. R. Sternberg, pp. 897–971. New York: Cambridge University Press.

Teleki, G. (1974). "Chimpanzee Subsistence Technology: Materials and Skills." *Journal of Human Evolution* 3, 575–94.

Terrace, H. S., L. A. Pettito, R. J. Sanders, and T. G. Bever (1979). "Can an Ape Form a Sentence?" *Science* 206, 891–902.

Toth, N. (1985). "The Oldowan Reassessed: A Close Look at Early Stone Artifacts." *Journal of Archaeological Science* 12, 101–20.

van Lawick-Goodall, J. (1970). "Tool-using in Primates and Other Vertebrates." In *Advances in the Study of Behavior*, ed. D. Lehrman, R. Hinde, and E. Shaw, 3, 195–249. New York: Academic Press.

van Sommers, P. (1984). *Drawing and Cognition: Descriptive and Experimental Studies of Graphic Production Processes*. Cambridge: Cambridge University Press.

Wynn, T. (1986). "Archaeological Evidence for the Evolution of Modern Human Intelligence." In *The Pleistocene Perspective Vol. 1*, ed. R. Foley and M. Day. Southampton: Proceedings of the World Archaeological Congress.

———— (1989). "The Evolution of Tools and Symbolic Behavior." In *Handbook of Human Symbolic Evolution*, ed. A. Lock and C. Peters. Oxford: Oxford University Press.

Index

Accommodation, 80

Acheulean: later, 19, 20, 66, 89–93; early, 26, 53, 87–89

Ad hoc technology, 63

Affine geometry: defined, 45; as a developmental stage, 57

Analysis and synthesis, 89, 94. *See also* Whole-part relations

Apes: compared to Oldowan, 81, 97; as having preoperational intelligence, 84–86, 89

Archaeology, viii

Assimilation, 80

Awls, 48, 49

Baseball, 73

Bifaces: bilateral symmetry of, 17–18, 20; minimal trimming on, 18; examples, 26–33 passim, 51–56 passim; and overall design, 60; on large flakes, 63

Biomechanical constraints, 81–82

Boundaries: defined, 14; on choppers, 14; and Oldowan tools, 23; mentioned, 82

Cartesian coordinates. *See* Coordinate axes

Children: and perspective, 38; drawing, 44, 49, 50, 59, 81; and Piagetian stages, 72

Chimpanzees, 63

Choppers, 10–13, 18, 41, 52, 59

Classes. *See* Classification

Classification: in concrete operational intelligence, 76, 95; lack in Oldowan, 84; in early Acheulean, 88; in Franco-Cantabrian art, 95

Cleavers: and straight edges, 26; evidence for parallel, 45, 47; as later Acheulean class, 88

Comparative studies, 71, 77

Concrete operational intelligence: defined, 76; compared to formal operational intelligence, 94. *See also* Operational intelligence

Congruency, 47, 50, 53, 54, 56, 61, 91–92

Conservation: and operational intelligence, 75; defined, 76; and early Acheulean, 87; and early *Homo sapiens,* 92

Constructivist approach: Piagetian theory as, 71

Continuity: as analysis and synthesis, 18; defined, 18; as whole-part relationships, 18, 19. *See also* Whole-part relations

Coordinate axes: and handaxes, 52; and euclidean space, 57, 61; mentioned, 26

Cores, 3, 11

Cross-cultural studies, 71, 96

Cross sections: defined, 28; and later Acheulean artifacts, 29, 32, 37, 38; and early Acheulean artifacts, 33, 37; as evidence of three-dimensional space, 61; as evidence of operational intelligence, 90; mentioned, 25, 51, 52

Decentration, 88–89

Developed Oldowan, 66

Diameter: as evidence of spatial interval, 40, 58, 60; on discoids, 41; on spheroids, 44

Discoids, 40, 41, 45, 52, 58, 60

A Note on the Author

Thomas Wynn is Associate Professor of Anthropology at the University of Colorado at Colorado Springs, where he has taught since 1977. He earned an A.B. from Occidental College in 1971, and a Ph.D. from the University of Illinois at Urbana-Champaign in 1977. His articles on the evolution of human intelligence have appeared in *Man,* the *Journal of Human Evolution,* and *World Archaeology.* This is his first book.